—THE
META-
HUMAN

—THE— META- HUMAN

A Handbook for Personal Transformation

by Paul Solomon

HAMPTON ROADS
PUBLISHING COMPANY, INC.

The masculine pronouns he, him, and his
are used in this book
primarily for the sake of convenience,
and are not meant to imply preference
for one gender over another.

Cover and book design by Donning Productions

Printed in the United States of America

I wish to express my deepest gratitude
for those who spent sleepless nights,
and gave dedication "beyond the call of duty,"
to help prepare this book for publication.
For assistance in reviewing, re-writing, and editing:
Jamie Tyson, Myrrh Haslam, Sharon Solomon,
Philip Rima, David Solomon, Stephen Haslam, Grace David,
Renee Bost and Angelica Roquas.
For the computer software programs that
streamlined the preparation of the manuscript,
special thanks to David Goedhart.

Paul Solomon

Contents

"You Can Be
More Than Average"

Preface

This is a book about love.

It is a book to bridge the gap between secular and religious descriptions of human consciousness and human potential. I sincerely believe that many valid tools of transformation and techniques of applied psychology have been appropriated by religion. I define religion as "man creating God in his own image."

Serious students of human potential and metaphysics often reject "out of hand" anything that smacks of dogma or religion. This may cause us to overlook some very useful tools.

Please note that for me, the words "Higher Self," "Creative Source," and God are interchangeable terms. "Inner Self Helper," "Christ" and "Living Love" are interchangeable terms. When the word "Love" in the text appears in caps, it is interchangeable with God or Christ.

Please don't make too much of religious connotations. This is meant to be a practical look at the Meta-Human. It is meant to inspire you to become all you can be.

Paul Solomon

CHAPTER I

The Average Human

Let me introduce you to The Average Human. There is another name for The Average Human; the Average Human is a victim. Average Humans are victims of the weather; they are victims of the attitudes, beliefs and responses of other people. Average Humans are victimized by government, by taxes, by authority figures and by their own belief systems.

LIVING IN VICTIM CONSCIOUSNESS

The Average Human believes that if he is happy, it is because of situations in his life that are pleasant. He can be happy if he has enough money, good health, a good job and if things are going well in his life.

The Average Human believes that if he is unhappy, it is someone else's fault. Someone or something has made him unhappy. The Average Human is not in control of his own life or emotions.

The Average Human does not know that happiness is a habit. He does not know that unhappiness is a habit.

If you place an average person in the best possible situation and circumstances, he will be happy — for a few minutes. Then he will find something to complain about and go back to his habit of being unhappy.

If you place a habitually happy person in the worst of circumstances, he may be unhappy for a short time. Then he will think, "Why should I be in this miserable situation and be unhappy too?" And he will return to his habit of being happy — even in the worst of circumstances.

The Average Human uses statements like, "You hurt my feelings," "She made me so angry," and "You certainly embarrassed me last night."

A LITTLE TEST FOR VICTIM CONSCIOUSNESS

What would happen if I encountered you on the street and called you stupid? What happens when someone hurls an epithet or an insult?

If you live in victim consciousness, it will change your blood chemistry.

If I would deliberately try to hurt you or insult you, I am, by definition, your enemy. If your enemy can change your blood chemistry by speaking a single word like "stupid," or a four-word phrase, like "you s.o.b.," then your enemy has more control over your emotions than you have, and you are, by definition, a victim.

THE TRUTH ABOUT VICTIM CONSCIOUSNESS

The truth is that no one has ever made you angry. No one has ever hurt your feelings or embarrassed you. It is not possible. Another person can say what he wants to say or do what he needs to do. If you don't like what he has said or done, you can be angry — if you want to! And you can choose not to be angry. The decision is yours. It always has been and always will be. No one else really has control over your emotions or well-being.

THE TRUTH ABOUT EMOTIONS AND FEELINGS

Emotions are not something that just happen to you. Emotions are something you do. Emotions are goal-oriented activities. You experience emotions or feelings to get something you want. Unfortunately, these goal-oriented activities seldom work. They often get you the opposite of what you wanted and make you feel bad, in addition to the failure to achieve a goal. That's being a "double-victim."

THE AVERAGE HUMAN IS HIS OWN WORST ENEMY

All humans think in conversation. There is a conversation going on in your mind right now. You are thinking. And you think by talking to yourself. You may use words, images, feelings or concepts but your thinking is a conversation. It is not a one-sided conversation. Your self-talk will typically argue between two or more points of view.

There is nothing wrong with talking to yourself. It is an appropriate way to think. What you tell yourself can make you powerful or weak. It can make you well or ill. Your self-talk can make you successful or cause you to fail. If you wish to use your self-talk to empower and support yourself, you will need to realize what you are telling yourself. And you will need to talk to yourself on purpose.

Behavioral research psychologists tell us that fully 75% of The Average Human's self-talk is negative, unsupportive and is actually destructive to his own self-interest.

YOU CANNOT STOP DOING WHAT YOU DON'T KNOW YOU ARE DOING

The Average Human does not even know the content of his self-talk. He does not know what he is telling himself about him-self, his future, his past or his own self-image. He cannot change his self-talk until he knows the content.

FURTHER FACTS ABOUT THE AVERAGE HUMAN

The average college graduate can read about 350-400 words per minute. It is possible to read 3,000-20,000 words per minute.

The average person has a poor memory, especially for names. It is possible to remember anything and everything of which you have ever been consciously aware.

The Average Human is not very prosperous. In fact, the Average Human is afraid of greed and afraid of money. The Average Human has been taught that money is the root of all evil and believes that there is something admirable about being poor. The Average Human will live his life at the same level of poverty or success as that established by his parents. The Average Human will avoid being a greater success than his father was.

THE AVERAGE HUMAN FEELS GUILTY

Humans have been taught that feeling guilt will make a person better. "When I have done something wrong, if I feel guilty enough, long enough, I will make myself better" is a common belief of The Average Human. This belief is so pervasive among Average Humans that it strongly influences our criminal justice system. Juries are more lenient if the defendant shows remorse. The belief is well established that guilt can make you better.

THE TRUTH ABOUT GUILT

A feeling of guilt serves a purpose. Its purpose is accomplished in about 30 seconds. The purpose of guilt is to make us aware of having made a mistake or having violated our own principles. A sense of guilt is useful to make us aware. Having accomplished this, guilt's effectiveness is finished. Extended guilt is a tool of punishment for self-flagellation.

Extended guilt does not make you better, it makes you weaker. If you feel guilty enough, long enough, you will lose the strength you need to avoid repeating the same mistake. Feeling guilty means you are going to do it again. A sustained feeling of guilt will impress you with the belief that your mistake is stronger than you are. It will cause you to believe that you deserve punishment and you will find a way to punish yourself. But The Average Human believes in guilt and punishment. The Average Human feels a responsibility to feel guilty.

THE UNIVERSAL RELIGION

The Average Human worships at the altar of a universal god. The god's name is fear. This universal religion has a distinct liturgy. It is an effective, although negative, practice of meditation. It is called worry. The Average Human is very devout; he worries every day.

The Average Human believes that responsible people worry. Parents, especially, worry. Good parents worry about their children. The Average Human worries about finances, the future, health, safety and anything else important to life. This negative meditation is effective because it constitutes a self-fulfilling prophecy.

THE AVERAGE HUMAN IS FEARFUL

The Average Human has been taught that it is wise to fear some things. The belief is that fear will protect. Average Humans believe that fear will help them to avoid what they fear.

THE TRUTH ABOUT FEAR

Fear weakens. It does not protect. Fear paralyzes. It does not motivate toward safety. Respect motivates toward safety. The wise person will study what he fears. The more he knows about what he is afraid of, the greater his respect for the danger. Respect is different from fear. Respect will allow appropriate response to danger. Fear actually increases danger. Fear is FAITH IN EVIL. It is another important part of the liturgy of the universal religion.

THE AVERAGE HUMAN LACKS SELF-CONFIDENCE

Humans have been taught that too much self-love leads to egotism. Humility is much prized and much misunderstood by The Average Human. A human who lacks self-esteem, self-worth and self-love will lack the confidence that is essential to success. Egotistical people are not people with too much self-love or self-worth, they are people who do not believe in themselves. Egotistical people swagger and brag to prove something they do not believe: that they are all right, that they matter, that they deserve special treatment. The egotist must receive special treatment in order to "belong." Egotists are Average Humans who are afraid they are not even average.

THE TRUTH ABOUT SELF-LOVE

People who love themselves are all right. People with self-love do not need to be "better" than others. Humans with self-love and self-esteem have self-confidence. A person with self-love can love others easily. Those who have self-love are not afraid of being unloved by others. Knowing their worth, people with self-love can love others with the confidence that their love will be returned.

THE AVERAGE HUMAN HAS STAGE FRIGHT

The Average Human is always afraid of making a fool of himself. He imagines that being before an audience will reveal what he really is: a bumbling fool. This belief about self is a self-fulfilling prophecy. The Average Human on stage is stiff, his fear is palpable, his body language and tongue-tied expression make an audience uncomfortable. Audiences are largely composed of Average Humans. People in an average audience are uncomfortable because they identify with stage-fright. They see themselves in the clumsy performer "making a fool of himself."

THE AVERAGE HUMAN IS A HALF-WIT

Recent theory suggests that the brain is hemispherically specialized: the left hemisphere of the brain is concerned with the rational, logical reasoning process and the right brain is concerned with intuitive, imaginative, inspirational thinking. The Average Human who is left-brain dominant is likely to be structured and decisive, but rigid. The Average Human who is right-brain dominant is likely to be spontaneous and flexible, but disorganized.

The Average Human has been taught that reasoning and logic are the only way to think. He is limited to "Aristotelian thinking." The Average Human was taught to throw away daydreams and imagination to become an adult. If a child speaks of a startling discovery, the average adult will ask, "How do you know?" If the child says, "I saw it with my eyes," or "I heard it with my ears," the adult is likely to believe him. If the child says, "A bunny rabbit told me," the adult will say, "That's just your imagination." The communication is that imagination is not a valid source of information. A child is obliged to quit daydreaming and using his imagination by the age of fourteen. Now he has discarded fully half his brain and is taught to function as a half-wit.

THE AVERAGE HUMAN IS DANGEROUS

There are approximately 4.5 billion Average Humans on the planet today. Average Humans live in victim consciousness. Victims live in fear, and victims are dangerous. People who live in fear lash out at any perceived threat. Insecure people can be vengeful, competitive and will do anything necessary to assure survival. The survival mechanisms of victims, insecure people or Average Humans are not always logical. Just as a frightened animal is dangerous, so is the frightened human.

War and crime are the products of Average Humans. The Average Human is easily persuaded of the necessity for war machines and for the protection of police powers. Frightened people are willing to kill for their beliefs and their lifestyles.

THE AVERAGE HUMAN IS AVERAGE

Perhaps the greatest misfortune of The Average Human is that his life will be largely wasted. It will not make a difference to history that he was alive. Humanity will not be affected by his passing. The Average Human will not contribute to society. It will not matter that he ever existed.

CHAPTER II

The Possible Human; A Question of Values

*"Only a handful have lived in such a way
as to be remembered individually."*

"THE POSSIBLE HUMAN"

That little descriptive phrase is used by Dr. Jean Houston[1] to conjure an image of what a human could be when exercising full potential.

Approximately 10.5 billion people have lived on this planet throughout recorded history. Only a handful have lived in such a way as to be remembered individually. A few men and women have been so effective that they precipitated a great leap forward in understanding and effectiveness for mankind. If each of the 10.5 billion was potentially a Possible Human, then history is tragic.

"For nearly one hundred thousand years, the brain remained hugely disproportionate to the work it was called upon to do....The potential mental capacities of an Aristotle or a Galileo were already anatomically and physiologically present, waiting to be used among people who had not yet learned to count on ten fingers. Much of this equipment is still unused, still waiting," says sociologist Lewis Mumford.[2]

WHAT IS THE POSSIBLE HUMAN?

The Possible Human is a person who redefines our beliefs about what is humanly possible.

Athletes at the International Olympic Games redefine what is physically possible every four years. Harry Lorayne in **The Memory Book** has demonstrated that The Possible Human has a phenomenal, near-photographic memory.[3] Evelyn Wood, the originator of Reading Dynamics, has shown that The Possible Human can read 2,000 or more words per minute; the average college graduate reads no more than 350 to 450 words per minute.[4]

Initiates of Hatha Yoga demonstrate that The Possible Human can control rates of circulation and respiration, pain perception, and other body functions usually considered involuntary.[5] C.G. Walter and Lyall

Watson write of the scientific evidence:

> "The conscious control of involuntary functions is common-
> place in yoga, Zen, and some African cults. Pulse rate, breath-
> ing, digestion, sexual function, metabolism, and kidney activity
> can all be influenced by and at will. [Some yogis] can slow the
> heartbeat almost to the vanishing point, reduce the body
> temperature to what would normally be lethal levels, and reduce
> their respiration to no more than one breath every few minutes.[6]
> The reflexes that normally make us shy away from intense pain
> can be diverted so that nails are driven through the limbs and
> spikes through the cheeks or tongue. And while this is being
> done, the sympathetic nervous system can be locally suppressed
> or stimulated so that bleeding is prevented or encouraged. The
> pupils, which normally respond to light and emotion, can simi-
> larly be controlled. Physiologists have [even] succeeded in doing
> such unlikely things as making their hair stand on end or their
> pancreas secrete more than the normal amount of insulin."[7]

British Admiral (retired) E.H. Shattuck has apparently demonstrated
the ability to regenerate cartilage of the hip joint and reduce enlargement
of the prostate gland using visualization and meditation techniques.[8]

Thomas Edison and Albert Einstein have demonstrated the kind of
mental creativity characteristic of The Possible Human. Edgar Cayce
showed us that there are no valid limits of the senses for The Possible
Human.[9] Moses and Jesus Christ showed us that the Possible Human
can accomplish things so spectacular that Average Humans consider
them to be miracles.

BARRIERS TO BECOMING A POSSIBLE HUMAN

If we all have such great potential, and if indeed some humans have
actually exhibited the abilities of The Possible Human, why are we still
expressing so little of our capacity? What stops us from becoming The
Possible Human?

THE POSSIBILITY CONDITIONING BARRIERS

THE PHYSICAL CONDITIONING BARRIER

Perhaps the greatest popular example of the conditioning barrier in
recent times was "the four-minute mile." Until 1954 it was a "demon-

strated fact" that no athlete could run the mile in less than four minutes. However, Sir Roger Gilbert Bannister believed the four-minute barrier was largely psychological. On May 6, 1954, Bannister ran the mile in 3 minutes 59.4 seconds at Iffley Road Track in Oxford, England. Since Bannister broke the barrier, about 300 others have duplicated or surpassed his feat.[10] A look at the evolution of the world record for running the mile is revealing:

1954 - John Landy, Australia	3.58
1957 - Derek Ibotson, Great Britain	3.57.2
1958 - Herb Elliott, Australia	3.54.5
1962 - Peter G. Snell, New Zealand	3.54.4
1965 - Michel Jazy, France	3.53.6
1966 - Jim Ryun, United States	3.51.3
1967 - Jim Ryun, United States	3.51.1

The conditioning barrier, it seems, never really lies shattered at the feet of The Possible Human. It rather yields by inches or seconds. It stands like a great wall just a fraction behind the latest record, waiting to be nudged again by the next Possible Human.

THE SOCIAL CONDITIONING BARRIER

The Possible Human pushes beyond the limits learned through social conditioning.

In the November 1984 issue of OMNI magazine, Barbara Rowes in "Fighting Chance" writes about a West Point woman cadet who, in 1983 "against all physiological odds scampered to the top of the rope, using only her hands."[11] Until then women had been compensating for their upper body weakness by using their legs as leverage. Tests given showed that the female cadets had only half the upper body strength of the male cadets. While it is still unclear what role social conditioning plays in female performance, Colonel James Anderson, director of the department of physical education at West Point, suspects "that society's paternalistic attitude toward women [has] greatly contributed to their limited physical performance." His tactic of not placating the women with a pat but treating them the same as the men "has affected a marked change in the response of the women," according to Rowes.[12] Dr. Robert Stauffer, director of research and evaluation at West Point, also comments in OMNI that if society continues to encourage women to perform at top levels, "I think the difference between men and women in such popular sports as running will probably narrow itself to three percent in terms of performance times."[13]

Sports psychologist Arno Wittig contends that men will also benefit from taking on such female traits as compassion. "Instead of women becoming more like men, it would be better if men showed more of what have been traditionally considered female strengths," he says.

THE PHYSIOLOGICAL CONDITIONING BARRIER

When we reach our "very real" physiological limits, we are forced to recognize that these are greatly influenced by our conditioning. We may even ask "Is the physiological barrier real?"

While the breaking of the four-minute mile revolutionized belief about the physical barrier, these are intriguing reports to further suggest possibilities beyond the physiological conditioning barrier:

> The art of "long-gom" in Tibet produces the ability to travel very rapidly across the inhospitable upland wastes of that country. The training includes living in complete darkness and seclusion for thirty-nine months of deep-breathing exercises. Alexandra David-Neel tells of seeing a monk from the monastery in Tsang, renowned for training in swiftness, in full flight. "I could clearly see his perfectly calm impassive face and wide open eyes with their gaze fixed on some invisible far distant object situated somewhere high up in space. The man did not run. He seemed to lift himself from the ground, proceeding by leaps. It looked as if he had been endowed with the elasticity of a ball and re-bounded each time his feet touched the ground."[14] It is said that one of these skilled walkers can cover a distance of over three hundred miles in about thirty hours — between sunrise on one day and midday of the next. That is an average of about ten miles an hour across all kinds of country by day and by night. Marathon runners, by comparison, travel at an average of twelve miles an hour, but only for just over two hours at a time on good roads.[15]

THE SACRIFICE BARRIER: A QUESTION OF VALUES

Perhaps the most valid barrier to full realization of The Possible Human is the sacrifice barrier. While it may be true that each of us can learn to read 3,000 words per minute, develop a phenomenal memory, and leap gazelle-like over great distances at high rates of speed, the evidence suggests that the training is available only at great sacrifice of time and effort. While the effects are highly desirable, the required training, concentration, commitment and persistence evoke images of the (presumed mythical) Mystery Schools of antiquity.

With this I will not argue. Every Olympic gold medalist and each of the great men and women of history achieved greatness at great sacrifice. It is also true, of course, that what they sacrificed is the stuff of which ordinary lives are made. Whether to invest the time, energy and commitment necessary to greatness is a question of values.

While the lives of The Possible Humans are spectacular as compared with The Average Human, there have been those who lived in such a way as to be considered spectacular by comparison even to The Possible Human. It is here that we encounter the barrier to becoming a "Meta-Human."

CHAPTER III

Introducing
The Meta-Human

THE "DIVINE" BARRIER

While not discounting the accomplishments of The Possible Human, they are hardly to be compared with miracles attributed to Jesus Christ or Gautama Buddha or Moses. The ultimate human perhaps falls into a third category that I call "The Meta-Human."[1]

At the mention of Jesus Christ, you may experience one of these self-limiting reactions to the divine barrier:

> 1. Jesus Christ was born God, born of a virgin, and naturally possessed abilities the rest of us don't have. In fact, to consider that we can do what He did may seem sacrilegious.

> 2. What Jesus Christ did has religious significance, but my interest is in practical, not religious matters.

> 3. The stories of Jesus Christ are mythical and superstitious and do not have historical validity, therefore they do not really represent abilities of The Possible Human or the Meta-Human.

An examination of these reactions may be very revealing, especially since they often apply, to some extent, to all the other examples as well. The first reaction is an almost universal "cop-out." It extends to Albert Einstein by our tendency to say "he was a genius" and to Edison by saying "he had special talent for inventing." Isn't it amazing how handy our excuses are for not accepting responsibility for potential? Jesus Christ actually said, "All these things I have done, you can do, and greater things than these" (John 14:12). He rendered invalid our excuse for not duplicating his accomplishment because of His special birth and circumstances, and yet it is somehow considered more religious to put Him on a pedestal and think it ridiculous that we could emulate Him. What is so worshipful about thinking that He lied? Either we can do the things

He is reported to have done, or He lied.

The second reaction would relegate His psychic abilities and miracles to the religious realm as separate from practicality. If, indeed, there is some technique of inducing healing spiritually, and if such techniques are more effective than those we now use, is it not practical to research the methods and end a religious/secular separation that is not serving us? Perhaps our whole philosophy of separation of spirit and matter is totally invalid.

The third reaction supposes that miracles are myth and deserve no research or attempt to duplicate. Indeed, this reaction extends not only to the accomplishments of Jesus, but even to Evelyn Wood, for example. Many people say that her techniques of speed reading are not valid. The objection is that speed readers are only "skimming" and not actually reading. It is interesting that skepticism is so often a mark of the "intellect." It is thought intelligent to doubt that these extraordinary abilities exist. Let's examine that:

Even if the skeptics are right, it is observable that many people are studying speed reading and are delighted with the result. By not assuming that it won't work they take advantage of a possibility automatically denied the skeptic, and they are delighted with the result. Now who is intelligent? Certainly many researchers have denied the possibility of "psychic diagnosis" as purportedly demonstrated by Edgar Cayce. It is, in fact, de rigueur in scientific and academic circles to even "pooh-pooh" research in these areas. And yet, while the skeptics deny and protest, many people attribute their healing to Cayce's efforts. What if they had allowed "intelligent skepticism" to prevent their seeking his help? In essence we could say "possibility" thinkers lose nothing and often gain enormously by considering the possibilities, and the "impossibility" thinkers deprive themselves of their birthright!

A NOTE ABOUT SKEPTICISM

There are two kinds of skepticism. There is healthy skepticism that considers and invites all possibilities without gullibility, and there is bigoted skepticism that denies any possibility that offers no proof of validity. This bigoted skepticism has cost our world centuries of evolution through persecution of possibility thinkers.

This is not just opinion. There is ample historical evidence that virtually every major new discovery in history was "pooh-poohed" by the scientific, academic and intellectual communities to the extent of organized attempts to punish and ostracize the pioneers. We certainly have enough examples of the destructive effect of this stupidity to call a halt to it as accepted practice in our time. Surely it is intelligent to consider the possibility that the miracles of the Bible are myth. It is also intelligent to consider the possibility that each reported incident may have some validity and to leave no stone unturned until we find whether such occurrences can be duplicated!

The very fact that each successive generation throughout history has had reports of psychic phenomena, miracle healings and other "miraculous" occurrences is ample reason to explore the possibilities with great vigor.

AN ASSUMPTION: A REASON FOR OUR BIRTH

Let's make an assumption that there is a reason for our being born. There is a purpose for life. It is observable that there are laws governing the cause/effect relationships on our planet. Those who discover how to produce the right causes benefit from the effects. Pain and ineffectiveness are the result of setting the wrong causes in motion. Producing the right causes leads to effectiveness and in fact a joyous, healthy life. This leads to two conclusions: that this planet is a school for learning correct causes; and that a joyous, happy, effective life is an ideal result.

We are assuming that life is a school, and that the lessons are demonstrated by wrong (uncomfortable, painful) results from wrong causes, and right (joyous, happy) results from right causes. This seems very simple until we consider the possibility of accidents and circumstances beyond our control. Just for experimental purposes, let's extend our assumption to suggest that there are no accidents or circumstances beyond the control of the Meta-Human. These phenomena, like miracles, are only effects of laws we have not yet understood. This has to remain a theory. We can't prove it until we become the Meta-Human. It is a theory, yet, that can work for us. It works by releasing our limitations and allowing us to work toward mastery over our environment.

I personally believe that you and I were perhaps ridiculously ambitious when we chose to live on this planet. I fantasize that from some vantage point beyond space and time we looked at this little planet with its cause/effect laws and thought, "How simple! I can create the right causes and produce very pleasant effects, thus mastering the challenges of that existence." We applied for permission to build an experiential unit (body with mind) and set about influencing the thoughts and actions of potential parents. We entered with the intention of mastering the laws. One who masters the laws of cause/effect relationships is called a Master. It seems to me that you and I entered here for no less purpose than to become a Master! Isn't that ridiculously ambitious?

From society's point of view that is ridiculous. In fact if I dare to voice the possibility that I could become a Master I will be condemned as an egotist and suspected of insanity. To consider the possibility that we can do what I believe we came here to do is discouraged, to say the least. Is it any wonder that so few do, in fact, accomplish it?

THE INNER GUIDING LIGHT

Those who have been most effective throughout history seem to have had some inner guiding light. In fact, many effective beings have spoken of their source of guidance and inspiration in just those terms, including Christ. Becoming conscious of, and using, an inner guiding light drastically alters our very method of thinking, our perception of reality, and indeed our consciousness. The discovery of a greater source of information and guidance is basic to the Meta-Human. If you do not have a blueprint you cannot build a house. If you do not have a light you cannot see in the dark. In the building of a life it is "inner light consciousness" that transforms the Average Human into a Meta-Human.

Perhaps the most important message of this book is not whether The Average Human should strive for greatness or transformation, but rather, that there is a choice. No one has to settle for being average. For those who do make a conscious choice to be Average Humans, I can only say, "Go with my blessing."

CHAPTER IV

Some Theories On Human Potential

"It amuses me that the proponents of each of these theories often attempt to discredit the others, although each contributes something meaningful to the whole."

There was a time in history when thinking was considered a process of asking God (or the gods) for information. Thoughts came through wondering and asking a question in a prayer-like process. Answers then came through waiting and listening.

ARISTOTELIAN THINKING

Then along came Aristotle who defined the process differently. He said thinking consists of making observations through the senses, storing the observations, then making comparisons and drawing conclusions. Aristotelian thinking became "the only way to think" so that eventually we began to say that imagination and inspiration are not valid techniques of thinking. This idea is so pervasive, in fact, that today we teach our children to discard all other processes and use only rational, logical, deductive, conclusive reasoning.

Surely history has shown that our greatest thinkers did not often make their discoveries through a rational, logical process, but rather by inspiration.

EDISON

Thomas Edison used some fairly drastic techniques to induce this inspirational thinking process. One technique included going for days without food and pacing the floor to do without sleep long enough to induce an altered state of consciousness. In this altered state, he would sit with a steel ball-bearing in each hand and relax until the ball-bearings slipped from his hands to the floor. At this point, he would pose a question and wait for the answer to come to mind. He theorized that "answers are in the air."

EINSTEIN

Albert Einstein spoke of sitting on his front door stoop and watching clouds drift until there was a sensation of movement or "swimmy-headedness." In this state, ideas would come.

SCHUMANN

The composer, Schumann, said that although his rational mind was trained in music theory and was capable of composing with his rational understanding of music theory, this was not the process he used for composing. Instead, he composed by "remembering a melody" as if it already existed and he would write what he heard from memory.[1]

CAYCE

Edgar Cayce used hypnosis to induce a deep trance state in which he could apparently diagnose illness and recommend effective treatment or cures. His technique is reminiscent of the Hebrew prophet, Daniel, who went to sleep to receive an accurate interpretation of King Nebuchadnezzar's dream.

MOSES

Perhaps the greatest example of psychic ability in history is Moses, the Hebrew prophet. Here is a man who accepted responsibility for a whole nation of people with no place to live, no organization or laws, not even such as existed in other nations of the period. To succeed at such a challenge is miraculous in itself, even if manuals and training for each step in organization had been currently available. Two things are exceptionally remarkable: the way he obtained his information, and the content of that information.

By Moses' own account, he went alone to a mountain top and talked with a voice coming from a light or a burning bush at the top of the mountain. The process was one of asking for information not available through a rational, logical process and listening for answers. The answers were especially remarkable because he was given instructions that were not scientifically validated until nearly three thousand years later.

The book of Exodus contains instruction in sanitation, sterilization, nutrition and epidemic control. The techniques he was given could have prevented the "black plague" in Europe centuries later, had they been applied. It was not until Ignaz Semmelweis[2] did his work in Austria just 100 years ago that what Moses wrote was discovered to have scientific basis.

Psychic research is difficult because information from a psychic must be tested to prove validity. If validity is easily proven, there is an over-stated assumption that the psychic could have known through some other means. In the case of Moses, we have information from a "psychic" or prophetic Source that was not discovered or proven from a rational source for at least two thousand years. There is an assumption, of course, that Moses studied in the universities of Egypt and brought his knowl-edge of medicine, organization and laws from that culture. That argu-ment is not sustained according to McMillan's book, **None of These Diseases,** which reports that a contemporary Egyptian book, **The Papyrus Ebbers,** contains the admonition, "for treatment of imbedded splinters, apply donkey dung." Donkey dung, of course, is likely to be full of tetanus spores so that while Israel was applying laws of sanitation and sterilization, Egyptian doctors were giving their patients lockjaw.[3]

It is almost impossible to discredit the idea that Moses had some "super-natural" Source of information. But even if we refuse to accept that possibility, we are left with the observation that what he wrote established a precedent that is followed today in the legal world, in three major religions that serve more than two thirds of today's world, and even in medicine! What a spectacular Meta-Human. There is obviously good reason to pay attention to how he got his information.

AN INVESTIGATION OF ESP

Several years ago, I attended classes briefly at Wayland Baptist College in Plainview, Texas. Our psychology professor, Dr. N.E. West was interested in parapsychology. He was approached one day by an elementary school teacher from Laredo, Texas. The teacher was an amateur hypnotist.[4] There were several underprivileged children in his classes who were malnourished and had behavior and learning disabili-ties and some were hyperactive. The teacher reasoned that hypnosis could help lengthen their attention span and improve their memories. So, with permission from their parents, he began class sessions with a relaxation exercise and conditioning suggestions. He noted improve-ment but discovered a "side effect" as well. It seemed that the children would often answer his questions before he asked them. There appeared to be some kind of ESP or telepathy at work. Dr. West was asked to investigate.

Taking some of his senior students to help with research, Dr. West began testing the children with standard ESP tests. At first, the children scored very high on the tests, but quickly became bored and scores returned to average or even below. In one test using a telephone book, children were asked to describe people selected at random, people that they had never seen. Again, the scores were initially high but declined on repetition of experiments. The researchers were stumped.

One day a student researcher was chased by a dog on his way to the school. On his arrival, children began to laugh and point and describe the incident. Someone theorized that the mind became quickly bored by the ESP cards and other experiments that became a pointless game. The mind did not have sufficient motivation to seek accurate answers. But an emotion-packed situation seemed to have a different effect. Instead of a telephone book, the researchers used a hospital roster, asking the children to try to be of help in diagnosis and healing. Now they had sufficient motivation for accuracy, believing they could actually help someone in need. According to researchers, their accuracy returned to and maintained a significant level. The school teacher's name was Jose Silva, and the incident gave birth to The Silva Method.[5]

I had occasion to use a Silva technique with my daughter. An unusually bright and talented child, she nonetheless had learning disabilities including dyslexia. At age thirteen, she read on a first grade level and had to attend a special school. One of her teachers commented that while her intuitive mind was exceptional in ability to create plausible stories and a fairy-tale world, her rational mind seemed unable to follow the logical computer-like process for recalling answers to test questions.

She and I tried an experiment. I suggested she create a room she liked. She chose a meadow with horses. We then created a library in her meadow that contained all the books she used at school. When test-time came, she could go into her "imaginary" library, open the appropriate book and take her test with an open book. She was delighted, especially because it seemed somehow like cheating. But there was one problem.

She could spot the answer in her "inner book," but she still had reading difficulties. So I suggested that if she couldn't read the answer from the book, she should bring her teacher into the library and ask the question. She was to put down the very first answer that came to mind after asking her a question. The technique was so successful that the teacher called me to the school to express her concern about how Sherry might be cheating. She had improved so much, so fast that it didn't seem possible without cheating. I explained what we had done and was invited to share the technique with other children. In each instance, we found dramatic results. One of the greatest thrills of my life was when my daughter brought home a "straight A" report card for the first time. I am not particularly concerned with good grades, but I was thrilled with her new self-image. The benefit showed in her behavior, her carriage and a new joy of life. She discovered herself to be all right.

THE INNER-BRAIN, OUTER-BRAIN THEORY

Some brain researchers explain that the primitive brain is more intuitive and the psychic flashes, hunches and survival oriented "miracles" that sometimes save lives are activities of this primitive part of the brain. Rather than a left-brain, right-brain phenomena, it could be described as an inner-brain, outer-brain phenomena.

According to this theory, traumatic situations may allow the thought process to occur at a more primal level so that decisions are made intuitively or instinctively, perhaps using senses akin to the apparent "super-senses" sometimes observed in animals. There is an ability to perhaps "smell" danger or to sense it in a way that is not extra-sensory but rather "hyper-sensory." Some support for this theory comes from the fact that most "super" humans had a traumatic experience that motivated their increased effectiveness. Mystics have described a "dark night of the soul," which precedes enlightenment. Edgar Cayce suffered an incapacitating illness that precipitated his being hypnotized; St. Paul described the trauma of participating in the martyrdom of St. Stephen; the prophet Daniel's life was threatened; Moses killed a man in a rage. The theory points out that in almost every instance, there was a period of desperation in which the individual cried out for some "super human" assistance, then discovered abilities that were apparently inherent.

THE CREATOR-CREATED THEORY

The late Dr. Harold Saxon Burr of Yale University discovered a surface electrical potential on the human body. He found that the tiny electrical charge would change before an illness, giving the appearance of prognostication. Of course, others theorized that this electrical change indicated a disease process already active, though not yet biologically evident, rather than prognostication. He further discovered that electrical changes also occur before an accident and may even indicate the specific portion of the body that will be involved. In his book, **Fields of Life,**[6] Dr. Burr introduces T-Fields (thought fields) and L-Fields (life fields), indicating that thoughts have field properties (the ability to affect objects or other fields at a distance without visible means of transference). In **Blueprint for Immortality,**[7] by Dr. Burr, and in **Design for Destiny,**[8] by Edward Russell, Dr. Burr's work is extended to suggest that an intelligence is present before birth that participates in "creating" the body. The intelligence that will inhabit the body is present and influential in forming its instrument of expression.

This theory describes a "cause intelligence" that knows how to make a body and knows how a body functions. This intelligence is not the result of the brain functioning but rather is the cause of the brain. The intelligence we identify with is seen as a "result" brain function, with its ability to gather information through the five senses, store the information and draw conclusions. Unfortunately, we are taught that this "result mind" is the extent of our intelligence, so that our belief system denies us access to the "cause mind" or "creator mind."

There is some evidence that such a "cause mind" exists. It is observable that some kind of intelligence knows how to regulate heart beat and how to create new, specialized living cells to replace dying ones. Some unconscious intelligence knows how to rally defense systems for attacking disease or physical trauma. Obviously, there is a greater intelligence co-existing with me in my body than I consciously control.

The "Creator-Created" theory suggests that The Meta-Human is one who goes beyond the "created" or "result" mind to use the "Cause" mind as well. One could assume that this "Cause" mind knew the purpose of this life and built specific strengths and weaknesses, likes and dislikes, abilities, inclinations and talents according to the soul intent. If this is so, one would do well to get in touch with this "Cause" mind to understand one's purpose in life and how to accomplish it.

THE RELIGIOUS THEORY

There are, of course, several variations of each of these theories, including the religious theory.

Perhaps the most intriguing concept is the fundamentalist Christian idea of the "new birth." Being born again is described as a process of inviting the Christ to enter the "heart" and become Lord and ruler of the life. The result of this new birth is that the "Son of God" (expression of God) becomes the Source of my thought and action. This theory is very akin to the "Creator-created" theory. If the mortal self is the result self and the cause of my life is an expression of God, then essentially the new birth is the act of contacting my Creative Source Intelligence and asking the "higher mind" to make my decisions from its greater perspective rather than depending upon the created mind with its limitation of sensory input and stored information.

THE SPIRITUALIST THEORY

The spiritualist philosophy suggests that guidance comes from the survival of the personality after physical death. This theory further suggests that the passage of the personality or consciousness from the limitation of physical, sensory reality allows it to have a less limited view of events — past, present or future. This less limited view then allows the departed personality to act as a kind of advisor or "spirit guide" to friends or those of kindred mind still in the flesh experience.

THE AKASHA THEORY

While the word Akasha (or Akashic Record) is a Sanskrit transliteration and the philosophy is associated with Hindu, the idea has a counterpart in most religions. As explained by Manly Palmer Hall[9] in a little booklet entitled **The Invisible Record of Thought and Action,** the theory suggests that the basic building blocks of matter (atoms, molecules and cells) are constantly in motion and constantly changing. Each new atom or crystalline formation is affected, more or less, by the electrical force-field in which it is formed. Each new building block replaces an older one and carries its "signature" so that memory is added to the impression of the moment. Because thought produces electricity and because electricity is tenacious of equilibrium, the force-field in which cells are born is affected by thought. According to the theory, this electrical field impresses the thought and emotion of a given moment onto the very building blocks of matter in the same way that the thought and action is impressed on the cells of memory in the human body.

To illustrate the theory, let us suppose I am now in a room. The walls, floor and ceiling of the room appear to be stationary,solid and not moving. The laws of physics suggest this is not so. The walls are, in fact, made of particles in constant motion; and these atomic particles are subtly changing their relationship to one another, which allows the decay process to occur. The manner in which these atomic and sub-atomic particles bond together to form molecules is influenced by the presence of electricity, magnetism and gravity.

I am thinking in this room. Each thought produces an electrical charge. The electrical charge of each thought is apparently unique. Highly emotional thoughts may carry a greater electrical charge. The atmosphere around me is also electrically charged. Electricity is tenacious of equilibrium, which means that any electrical charge I produce within the charged atmosphere around me will affect that atmosphere throughout. Because molecules are being formed within that atmosphere, the effect of my thought on the atmosphere will subsequently affect the molecules being formed. Thus, the molecules will carry a record of my thought.

Brain research has revealed that a memory embracing a scene of many miles or a long period can be stored in a single microscopic cell. The process of storing memory appears to have no time/space limitation. The Akasha theory suggests that through a similar process, whole blocks of space, time, thought and action can be released again in a manner similar to remembering.

Through a process called "psychometry," a sensitive person can touch a physical object and by successfully avoiding rational thought, "remember" facets of its history. Perhaps no one knows precisely how we remember. It has something to do with association. By a process of an associated thought, we can direct the electrical activity of the brain to the particular cell in which a memory is recorded. The scene, emotion or idea is then released through "subtler senses." We "see" the scene with our subtler sense of sight, not with the optic nerve, or we "hear" the melody but not with the tympanic membrane.

Apparently, the psychometrist accomplishes an association by touching an object, and the "seeing" or "hearing" is accomplished in a manner similar to memory.

Edgar Cayce refers to "The Great Akashic Record" as "the skein of time and space"[10] in the fabric of the universe. According to this theory, a sensitive mind could "tune in" by an associative process to the idea behind the universe and receive universal guidance and prophecy.

THE ASTROLOGICAL THEORY

Astrologers reason that relationships between bodies of matter could scarcely avoid having some effect on universal equilibrium. Thus, the energies available at a particular place within the universe at a given moment are somewhat predictable by noting the relationships of the greater bodies to one another. Whether the conclusions drawn about particular heavenly relationships are valid is a matter for observation and research. The cycles of the moon have clear and measurable influence in nature, from the ebb and flow of the tides, to the age-old farmer's knowledge of planting while the moon is just at or before a waxing moon, in order to increase early plant growth. Many surgeons will not operate during the full moon because of a noticeable increase in blood loss, a fact that has been known for centuries by women in the menstrual cycle. If the moon has such important influence on our lives, it might be wise to study the effects of other heavenly bodies. It may be true that astrologers often depend as much on intuition as on accumulated data and observation, although the same could be said of many medical doctors.

WHICH THEORY TO BELIEVE

It amuses me that the proponents of each of these theories often attempt to discredit the others, although each contributes something meaningful to the whole. It seems as great a mistake to become caught up in one theory to the point of rendering the others unbelievable as it would to disregard them all. They are not mutually exclusive in any instance and the acceptance of one or all of them does not preclude scientific logic.

Any intelligent person must realize that we need all the help we can get in facing the complexities of our modern world. If I can use my intuitive, imaginative faculties to supplement my logical ability, I need not assume that doing so precludes my believing in assistance from a Divine Source within or beyond me. As Jean Houston purports in her book, **The Possible Human,** that if trauma can drive my decision-making process from the cerebral cortex to the brain stem, then perhaps by "dis-inhibiting the cerebral cortex"[11] through such techniques as used by primitives and aboriginals, I can reach that same thinking source. Is that considered "non-religious?" Certainly not, if my God created that ability. Do these processes preclude my speaking with a friend or loved one no longer physically living? Scarcely anyone who has lost a loved one did not "feel" or sense that person sometime later. How could they not be influenced by communication with someone they love? Or was my love limited to a physical body? As for psychometry, who has not entered a room where something felt wrong, a foreboding feeling or some such response?

The Meta-Human is one who refuses to settle for the limitation of five senses and a "result" mind. If there are other sources of awareness, one cannot afford to dismiss them through prejudice or dogma.

THE SIDDHIS

From every culture throughout history come stories of men or women with ability to heal others, to walk on water, to "teleport" themselves over great distances, to levitate, to regulate heartbeat and respiration and several other feats that range from amazing control to outright violation of physical laws as we understand them. Eastern writers have called these phenomena "siddhis" and declare that such abilities result from an inner transformation. Stories abound of the curious wanting to learn "how to do it." Intrigued with a particular feat of apparent magic, they approach a "holy man" asking to learn how to heal or how to levitate.

The teachers have consistently responded that such abilities are a RESULT. Not to be sought as an ability or a technique for its own sake, they are part of a whole, and one must develop that whole to experience the part. While it may be possible to teach one or another of these abilities as a technique, the teachers declare that to learn it this way would be destructive.

To the uninitiated, that may sound like doubletalk. Indeed, even the greatest teachers and gurus have often been accused of being secretive and selfish for not sharing freely their understanding and their intriguing abilities. Still, it is not so difficult to see the sense of this warning.

A STORY TOLD BY A FAMOUS GURU

A young man came to the guru and with great sincerity declared, "I really want to serve the world. There is so much need in the world, so much suffering. I would be willing to give my whole life and all that I have. Just please give me an ability to serve." The guru asked him, "What would you have me give you?"

He replied, "Grant to me a great gift of healing. I know I can encourage healing in others by loving and causing them to feel loved. I know that I can touch them with soothing strokes and even change the hemoglobin count of the blood with therapeutic touch.[12] But the need is so great and these methods are so small. I know you can teach me to simply touch and think 'Be healed,' and they could be healed instantly. Please teach me the ability to heal instantly by touch. Give me the great gift of healing."

"I looked into the young man's eyes," said the guru, and saw a great sincerity. As far as he understood himself, his intent was truly to serve. Yet his weaknesses were just as apparent. The very nature of his question showed that he was full of need and unfulfilled. His character had not been perfected."

The guru continued, "I looked forward into the possibilities that time could unfold. I saw the young man healing one after another. Dozens of people came, then hundreds. Word spread quickly and soon he was overwhelmed with the clamor of the crowd. He was soon surrounded by a worshipful clutch of followers who began to shield him from the crowd and worry how tired he was becoming. His sense of importance grew in great leaps. He began to develop a restlessness and grew more fond of being admired, worshipped and cared for than of serving the people. He grew lazy and required more and more money, then more power and admiration. He eventually became power mad and dominated the government. He became cruel and, finally, was assassinated."

"I saw other possible futures," the guru said. "In one, he was declared to be of the devil and was mobbed by fanatics. In another, he was acclaimed a holy man of the church. He built around himself doctrine and dogma that prevented unbelievers from approaching. People were not healed anymore."

The guru added, "The other possibilities were increasingly destructive, and I knew I would not grant this cruel wish even if I could. The young man turned away in anger assuring others that I am selfish and even a fraud rather than a teacher. He went out sowing seeds of hate that were far less cruel than would have been the effects of granting such a gift."

If a serious student were to approach such a teacher, not inquiring "how to do it," but rather asking for assistance in finding peace, in knowing love, or in seeking to learn how to serve, the teacher would begin a process that leads to transformation. The training can be stated as a formula that we call the Meta-Human Formula.

CHAPTER V

The Meta-Human Formula

CURRICULUM

A teacher initiates the Meta-Human formula through a process of character building, which is the basic building block of a secure, whole life. He would not talk of "how to be psychic" or "how to heal and levitate," but the steps of building strong character would cause a process of total transformation to begin.

The student would develop new concepts regarding himself and the basic factors that make life what it is. He would begin to take charge of his own life, his own self-image, and his own sense of fulfillment. The student would soon quit blaming others for his feelings, and would cease being a victim of circumstance. He would no longer be able to experience helplessness. Emotions would become choices, and the student would motivate himself, rather than requiring external deadlines and pressure to provide the needed motivation for accomplishment.

As confidence, security and clarity grow within the student, the need to hide behind a false self-image vanishes. Commitments

Corresponding Results:

1. Character building

2. Perception of reality without distortion

3. Responsibility for self is absolute

4. Self-acceptance and self-love equals fulfillment

5. Mastery of emotions

6. Fulfillment produces absolute honesty

become sacred vows, and the student's very word becomes a commitment. The qualities of kindness and caring, acceptance and understanding, and challenge and service combine to create a love that is strong and unconditional.

Life energies would begin to obey him. Pain and tiredness would respond to his command. Soon he would make friends with his body processes: the heart, the lungs, other organs and the immune system would respond to his direction. The student would not be taught to "overrule" the body processes but to gain their cooperation. Brain integration would soon develop by balanced use of both hemispheres, allowing brain and mind transcendence. It would become as if "heaven opened and the angels of God [were] ascending and descending upon the Son of man."[1]

All forces and laws of nature become recognized as "angels" or "devas," or, in Native American terms, the "Bosses" or "Grandfathers" of nature. These forces become available as servants to the same "one force" (Love/God) that the student (initiate) serves. The new initiate develops the sensitivity necessary to detect the subtler life/energy fields about the body, and the abilities to harness and use them. His influence extends deliberately beyond the confines of his corporeal structure.

7. Integrity is absolute

8. Unconditional love manifests

9. Mastery of the body's life force

10. Perception of reality beyond illusion (maya) produces brain integration and transcendence

11. Receiving of communication from angels (messengers of God)

12. Initiate sees God "face to face" (Peniel Experience)

To the new initiate, it no longer seems phenomenal to levitate or to "be somewhere else" suddenly without obvious means of transport. But certainly this new initiate is not inclined to "perform" such feats for entertainment, personal profit or ego satisfaction. There is a lack of any need to prove the siddhis. Character building has taught a new set of values. To have learned the "parts" (siddhis) without the whole would have resulted in a deprivation of the experience of whole life. That is why the teachers say that to learn the siddhis without transformation is to learn damnation. One is damned to settle for a false value at the expense of true value.

NOT JUST AN EASTERN CONCEPT

The concept of the siddhis is not just an Eastern idea. The third chapter of The Gospel of St. John tells a story that might be taken directly from an Eastern text. A man approached Jesus, wanting to learn how to "perform the siddhis." The man was a lawyer and a religious scholar. He began his conversation, "Master, we know that you are a teacher sent from God because no man can do these miracles (perform the siddhis) that you do, except God be with him." Jesus answered, "Unless you be born again [transformed], you cannot see the kingdom of God."

It can be argued that the "kingdom of God" is the realm in which spiritual principles rather than physical laws apply. He seems to be saying, "If you really want to understand these miracles, you'll need to be able to see into another dimension." In fact, His further explanation bears this out: "That which is born of flesh is flesh." The senses of the flesh are matter. They are designed for sensing matter. They are born of result and can only see result.

"That which is born of spirit is spirit." You will need spiritual senses to see causes. "The wind blows wherever it will" and you can hear the sound of it but you cannot detect its source or cause. You can see the trees respond to it, but that is a result. You think you have seen miracles, but what you actually saw was the effect of the wind. You saw the result of what happened. What actually occurred happened in a spiritual realm, in another dimension. The physical was changed in response to it. This appears to be a profound explanation of healing and, indeed, the effect of spirit on matter. By using the illustration of wind and how it is perceived, He seems to be saying, "What you saw and what I did are really two different things. You saw a physical change which you perceived as healing. I induced a spiritual cause which resulted in a physical change. You did not see the spiritual action."

Two principles need to be learned here. Mental/spiritual activity has a profound and often immediate effect on matter, and a subtler set of senses to perceive spiritual activity can be developed.

CHAPTER VI

Twice-Born

"The transformation experience did not seem at all like a graduation, but like an initiation, a beginning of a quest."

THE TWICE BORN

Perhaps we can construct in practical terms a scenario of the transformation or "new birth" process.

It would appear that there is a profound intelligence involved in the creative process. While some activities in gestation, involving cell replication of the fetus are explainable in chemical terms, there remain unexplained some crucial creative decisions apparently made in bringing about a human life with individuality and self-consciousness. In religious terms, we recognize that God is involved in this life-giving process. The religionists would say that Creative Intelligence is intimately involved in every step of development of the fetus and indeed will continue with the body throughout life. The creative process never stops.

This ever-present creative intelligence is not a human ability and yet it is so intimately intrinsic within the individual that it can hardly be "all that God is." Nor can it be separated from the identity of the individual. It could very well be referred to as something "born of God" which gave birth to and sustains man. It could be referred to as "God in man," which, in turn, makes of the body a temple or dwelling for the "God-presence."[1]

THE INNER SELF HELPER

The existence of an "indwelling presence" has apparently been validated by Jungian research analysts. Dr. Jean Shinoda Bolen describes what happened when Jungian analysts worked with cases of "multiple personalities," similar to those described in the books **The Three Faces of Eve** and **Sybil.** The researchers found that there may be several separate and distinct personalities living in a single body. Of these separate personalities, one may be male, another female. One may be old and others still children. Perhaps the most startling and interesting discovery was that one personality in a body may be diabetic while other personalities in the same body are not!

In their attempts to integrate the separate personalities, the researchers in each case discovered still another personality that was non-assertive. This non-assertive personality has interesting characteristics. In addition to being non-assertive, this personality is also loving, non-judgmental, and was not inclined to "cast out" or even reprimand other personalities in the same body. This non-assertive personality appeared to be the only personality which was aware of all the other personalities in the body. Other personalities were likely to think of themselves as the "real, inherent" personality of the body.

The non-assertive personality was asked if "it" could help to integrate the multiple personalities. "Yes," was the response,"but only if all the personalities agree to be integrated." This non-assertive personality was labelled, "The Inner Self Helper." The Inner Self Helper seemed to have natural healing abilities and was, by nature, always loving, gentle and helpful. This exciting discovery of an "Inner Self Helper" may validate the ancient teaching of a "higher self" or an inner "Christ" or "Holy Spirit." The researchers, in fact, asked if this Inner Self Helper is "God within." The response was affirmative, at least to the extent that the Inner Self Helper described itself as being "like" God within or the nature of God within.

If we identify this creative intelligence with God or see it as a "child of God" or a link with God, then it is likely that it either knows the "mind of God" or is able to commune with that Greater Mind. Some metaphysicians refer to this creative intelligence as the higher self or the higher mind which knows, "what I was made for and how to accomplish it."

A similar concept stated in somewhat less religious terms suggests that "my mind comes from somewhere." However I explain the biological basis of life, I have a measure of intelligence. I have a mind. The source of my mind must be a greater mind. Even if I don't choose to express it in religious terms, it is likely that this "greater mind" knows some things that I don't yet know. Carl Jung postulated a "universal unconscious mind," and the same idea has been extended to postulate a universal "superconscious," a reference to a collective higher mind or intelligence influencing individual intelligence.

PHYSICS, GENETICS AND THE DNA

Geneticists in our generation have discovered a wonderful little chain of protein called the DNA molecule which appears to carry the "code" of programming pattern which will determine such things as the sex, color of hair and eyes, and even the strengths and weaknesses and habit patterns of the individual. Genetic theory has even gone so far as to suggest that this brilliant little genetic code will manipulate the survival mechanism of the individual, putting its own survival interest above that of the greater body.[2] The somewhat distressing theory suggests that all actions and even choices are pre-programmed for the individual at the time of birth. It is a science-propagated predestination theory.

It seems to me that there is nothing so foolish as the argument between science and religion. If religion is valid, every scientific discovery will further our understanding of God and His universe. If religion is not valid, our dedication to our beliefs is inappropriate. Science, on the other hand, is foolish to argue with religion. Obviously, scientific discovery represents only what we have so far been able to understand, leaving a vast body of discoveries yet to be made. If there are no further discoveries not yet understood, research is certainly an expensive waste of time. To make science a dogma is to suggest that we cannot or must not act upon energies or opportunities not yet proven. We must sit and wait for replicated experimentation.

The historical fact is that religion has often discovered through faith what science proved correct several hundred years later. The reverse is also true. Science has sometimes corrected perception held by religion (as in the case of Galileo) to the mutual benefit of both. We now have sufficient historical data to demonstrate the benefits of cooperation between these disciplines in further understanding our universe and our challenges.

Modern physics is rapidly approaching a merger with ancient metaphysical ideas. The description of the atom as charged particles in constant motion was written thousands of years ago in Sanskrit. The current theories of creation sound very much like Kabalistic[3] texts. Burr's discovery of life fields and the genetic code theories add credence to a creative intelligence involved in the process of giving life.

BUT WHAT OF THE PREDESTINATION THEORY OF GENETICS?

Doesn't the genetic code destroy even the remote possibility that I can become a Meta-Human? What if that is not written or programmed into my code? Are geniuses predestined? Am I forced to be average because of my pre-programming?

I asked geneticist Dr. Derald Langham[4] to examine the data on which the "predestination" theory of genetics was based. His assessment delighted me. According to Dr. Langham, the specific programmed code does not preclude any possibility. It appears that the entire "catalogue" of possibilities is available to any individual. While there is apparently an intelligence involved in programming the computer-like DNA molecule, there is evidence to suggest that the resulting individual may very well respond in ways not totally characteristic of that programming. He may well fail to live up to the potential so available, or he may choose to rise far beyond what could be expected with his "programmed code."

SO THAT'S THE FIRST BIRTH; WHAT ABOUT THE SECOND?

There is a theological argument about the inherent nature of man. One school quotes Scripture, "In sin did my mother conceive me,"[5] and suggests that man is inherently sinful, a "lowly worm." The other school is horrified by such self-deprecation and says, "Man is an expression of God and his true nature is God-like." These are such opposite beliefs that surely one must be wrong.

It appears to me that when one flatly rejects what another has found to be valid, it is usually a mistake. Whether or not he adopts another's point of view, he will very likely learn a great deal by trying to understand why the other believes it. When a whole segment of the world population accepts an idea to the point of making it dogma, it is likely that some intelligent person made an original valid point. However distorted it may have become in the dogmatic process, there is usually something to learn in understanding how it came about.

Surely the apostles had a valid reason for describing man as a sinful, lowly worm. Yet the argument that man was made in the image of God and that his inherent nature must be God-like is also defensible through the same Bible. How can we reconcile the paradox?

We already have laid the groundwork in speaking of the Higher Self. We would even say there are two of you: a cause you and an effect you. A Creator/created or a real you and a false you. This theory suggests that before birth there was a purposeful design. There was an expression of God that built a body for a divine purpose.

WHY DIDN'T THAT HAPPEN?

Again there are various theories about the why. A fundamentalist theory says that the original "fall" of Adam destined that the rest of us should be born sinful and separated from our Cause self. Or you can explain it simply biologically. The physical body began to develop biological, electrical thinking processes at birth (or before). Through the reactions of others and through its own information storage process, this body-mind developed self-consciousness and identity. Even though the greater mind was available to be drawn upon, the process of learning to deal with the physical body and material world was a body-mind process. The individual gained his self-consciousness through the processes of the result mind and through the beliefs of society around him. Thus he identified with a result and not a cause.

THE HIGHER SELF HYPOTHESIS

There was a "potential you" before you had a physical body. That "you" was an expression of God, a child of God, a part of His perfect plan. That "you" was a co-creator with God and knew how to make a body. It knew how to do the "will" of God with a brain capable of thinking. This brain-mind was designed to process information about a material world and to operate a biological organism. Both the body and the brain-mind were results of your creative action. They are not you. They never were you. They are both results of you.

Then your physical body was born. Its brain-mind began to make observations and store images and ideas. You were born into a world with limited perception of reality. In a physical world with physical senses, you began to perceive matter as reality; in fact, others related to your body as if it were you. People began to describe you and react to you in specific ways: "He's so cute," "She's so smart," "She's stubborn." These descriptive phrases then began to form your personality and self-image. Soon, you put together your body and your personality and said, "This is me!" But it isn't you. It never was you. The identity you accepted was result of you.

This misperception in point of identity could be described as "the fall." The "you" that you identified with is a very limited being, programmed by society and prone to failure and misperception. Perhaps this false self is the "lowly, sinful worm" the apostles speak of. Surely it is at war with the "Meta You." The ego is identified with this false, limited, personality self. The possible you exists only as an inner potential. Who hasn't experienced a "still, small (but persistent) voice" inside communicating an almost nagging feeling that "I am more than flesh and blood." Something inside wants to be born and to live a fuller, greater life.

But new birth also means death. It means death of limitation and even the death of the false identity. The ego dies hard. The false self is at war with the possible self. And even more so with the Meta-Self. It feels like (and is) a life and death struggle.

THE CONVERSION EXPERIENCE OF NEW BIRTH

It has been observed, even by "non-believers," that the simple decision to accept Love, to accept Christ, can produce a greater sense of peace and reconciliation of conflict in a person than years of therapy. I know this to be true in my own experience of the phenomenon.

1953, Fort Worth, Texas. I was fourteen years old. My father was pastor of Immanuel Baptist Church. I was growing up in a home in which the highest communicated value was a personal relationship with God. There was daily prayer and Bible reading in the home and a strong sense of the omnipresence of God. Jesus Christ seemed accepted and an ever-present family member.

While this may be comforting at some times, I was overwhelmed with guilt, self-condemnation and unworthiness. Every idle thought, unkind act or encounter with newly discovered sexuality became another reason to torment myself, ask forgiveness and seek a verifiable relationship with God.

From time to time, my father had his preacher friends and fellow seminarians in our living room for special late-night prayer meetings almost as other men might gather for poker. I had no doubt that they invoked a very tangible presence of God. They laughed, cried and praised God with great shouts along with their prayers. I longed to enjoy it as they did but it rather invoked terror in me. It was not terror of God. It was a terror of my "condition" of being "lost" as they referred to it. It was a terror of being rejected by God.

One night, I had gone to bed and was awakened by the sounds and vibrant energy of one of these prayer meetings. I felt as if the atmosphere were permeated with an intense energy I would characterize as electrical. It seemed so tangible I scarcely dared move for fear of encountering a shower of sparks. The terror welled up and I sobbed, begging forgiveness and begging to know God. I suddenly realized that I was not in my bedroom at all. I was standing on a dirt road at the edge of a great field. It was fresh after a rain and there were woods in the distance.

Rising like a great column on the horizon, I saw a great cloud-like figure. I suddenly heard myself shout, "God! You're my God!" Just as suddenly I found myself sitting up in my bed alarmed that I may have awakened the whole house. I noticed my brother still sleeping soundly in his bed in the same room. I cannot say that the vision was the catalyst for the realization. It seemed more as if my acceptance of God as my own was the catalyst for the vision. It does not even seem to me that the vision was a necessary confirmation of the acceptance of the realization. It was enough in itself. The moment produced in me an undeniable, experiential realization that "God is mine and I am His." The more profound realization was that while I had waited for God to accept me, responsibility was mine to accept God. It was an early lesson in personal responsibility.

Perhaps the most enduring result of the experience has been a solid, undeniable and "unshakable" knowledge of a real and living presence of God that is not dependent upon belief. I have found that the experience did not confirm (or deny) the religious doctrine and dogma I had been taught, but rather began a quest for knowledge and understanding.

As for "transformation," the experience certainly imparted a sense of peace in my relationship with God. It allowed a vital transformation to self-acceptance and certainly imparted a previously unknown confidence in relating to others which, I am sure, allowed me to be more loving. It resolved my immediate conflict with guilt and lack of self-worth, and even ensured that I did not consider subsequent feelings of guilt to be overwhelming or threats of doom.

What I found myself unable to sustain was a sense that I had permanently and consistently allowed the Christ to be "Lord and absolute ruler of my life." This, I found, was a moment by moment challenge. This transformation experience did not seem at all like a graduation, but like an initiation, a beginning of a quest.

THE MOMENT OF DECISION

If there is a "false" me with a limited perspective, habits and belief systems that are not in my own best interest, and if I have been using that limited, false self to run my life, then surely I should not hesitate to look for a possible alternative.

If there is, also, a limitless Creator-self with a greater perspective and wisdom, a "Possible" me, born of God, and if there is a greater mind available to me to make my decisions and run my life, the decision should be simple.

The decision, perhaps, is simple. The total transformation process may take a lifetime. Remember that a belief is not a belief unless "you believe it." I am sorry if that sounds like double-talk but remember, I have believed that I am this body with its personality, habits and beliefs. I am identified with that. To recognize that there is a greater Possible Me with a greater mind and limitless abilities sets up a dichotomy. The dichotomy is not real if the "false" self is not real. Yet it is none the less perceived as real. I have created in my conscious perception a difference between what I have known myself to be and what I can become.

There is quite a difference between perceiving that there is a greater mind and transferring my thought process to actually think with that greater mind. To think with the greater mind would transform my very identity. I must first develop some point of reference for what the greater mind is like. I must begin to communicate with it and develop familiarity. I must begin to call on the greater mind to make decisions. I will begin to depend more and more on that greater mind for my thought processes until the greater proportion of my thinking originates there. The point of enlightenment comes when the lesser mind dies of disuse and the greater mind is my source of thought.

Great men of history have often written of the struggle on the path to transformation. It was after his great flash of illumination that St. Paul wrote, "The good that I would, I do not, and that I would not, I do." And he described the transformation process by saying, "I (the false) am crucified with Christ, nevertheless, I (the greater) live, yet not I (the false) but Christ (the child of God) lives in me." Still, he said, "I die daily," indicating the struggle of the false self to compete for life.

THE CHRIST WITHIN AND THE HISTORICAL JESUS

Here, again, is a great theological debate. There are those who believe that the Christ we should invite to become the Lord and ruler of life is the historical Jesus. Others say that Jesus demonstrated the Christ and is an example and a teacher rather than a mystical Savior. The argument even becomes bitter around the statement of Jesus, "I am the way, the truth, and the life. No man cometh to the Father but by me." The idea that this one being could establish Himself, personally, as the only way is thought by some to be the absolute limit of dogma and even ego. Some explain the statement away by saying that what He really meant was that the only way is truth, etc.

Actually, the statement is both sensible and helpful in the context of what He taught. A sensible understanding of Jesus and what He taught will require us to consider Him in the time, place and context in which He presented Himself, as a Rabbi, teaching Judaism. He did not refute Judaism but presented Himself as a Jewish Rabbi, consistently, right up to His death and beyond. Even His disciples continued to teach in the Synagogues. The principle tenet and the watchword of Israel was and is, "Hear, O Israel, the Lord, thy God, the Lord is One." In this context of One God, He presented Himself as One with God and declared that the only way to live in total harmony or to express limitlessly (to enter the Kingdom of Heaven) is to be one with God and, of course, one with Him. If He was One with God. He could not possibly teach "At-one-ment with God" and be an example of it and still suggest that one can be one with God and not be one with Himself.

Does this make Jesus any less God? Certainly not. You can't be any more God than one with God. Does this mean that Jesus was no different than you or I? It means He was very different unless you and I have so completely lost separate identity as to be totally one with God. But wasn't He born divine and a Son of God from birth? Yes, but so were you, according to His teaching. Jesus said, "Don't you know who you are? I have said, You are gods and children of God."[6] Jesus was referred to as "The first fruits of them that slept."[7] The statement obviously meaning the first of us to wake up to who we really are and can be. The first Meta-Human and no less divine.

Then can I ask the historical Jesus to be my Lord of life? Why not? If you call on the historical Jesus Christ, you are calling on one who is supposed to be one with (same as) the consciousness of God. If you seek your Higher Mind, you seek the expression of God that is the Source of you. They are one and the same.

What if I do not believe in the historical Jesus but want to identify with my Higher Self and experience transformation? I do not believe that Jesus has an ego problem. If He is one with the Source of your mind, thought and life, and you accept that you are one with the Source, you have accepted Him whether you are attracted to the historical account or not. In fact, one need not be religious in the traditional sense at all to make practical use of this Source of mind. It would appear that it is a practical working reality and making it into a dogmatic religion is the work of "result-men" (a collection of false selves).

THE AVERAGE HUMAN OR THE META-HUMAN: A CHOICE

This is a time of "either/or" thinking. There are a number of books, workshops and seminars that concentrate on physical and mental development but avoid the idea of transformation. There are others which focus on spiritual transformation but consider "speed reading" and "memory training" a waste of time. The growth movement is effectively divided into two camps: those who have a type of behavior modification and pop-psychology tools for every social need while keeping both feet on the ground, and those who are so heavenly minded they are of no earthly use.

A master is, by his very nature, whole. A master is unique. He is as at home in the intellectual world and the practical work-a-day world as in the temple or the ashram. In this age of specialization the very idea of excelling at all facets of human potential may seem impossibly absurd.

But this book has not been written for the average person.

CHAPTER VII

Here There Be Dragons

"The greatest danger you will ever face is fear."

There is no worthwhile pursuit that is devoid of danger. When we speak of altered states of consciousness, establishing new belief systems, and accepting responsibility for power, we must acknowledge that there are dangers of misuse or misunderstanding. It is also true that we already live in a world in which these powers, tools and energies exist. If there is anything more dangerous than learning about these laws, it is failing to understand them. We cannot afford to be uninformed about the world in which we live.

Ideally, the study of transformation and the Meta-Human should be undertaken with the personal supervision of a well-informed guide. While such teachers are rare, they are not impossible to find. The purpose of this study is not to act as a do-it-yourself guide to enlightenment. It is rather an attempt at a definitive overview of the path to enlightenment. It is meant to be comprehensive enough to stimulate the student to seek while being informative enough to avoid costly mistakes. It is intended to intrigue and to motivate you. It is intended to suggest what is possible. It may even assist as a guide to the qualified teacher or study group leader. Use it wisely. Be informed. Study the reference material. Be responsible.

THE POSSIBLE DANGERS

In this chapter, I will point out possible dangers and common points of misunderstanding. I will attempt to give well-placed warnings without arousing fear. Keep in mind that the words of warning will often be understated because to arouse fear is to increase danger. The greatest danger you will ever face in growth is fear.

THE FEAR DRAGON

When one reads the accounts of mystics and shamen, those who have explored deeply into self, altered states of consciousness and spiritual growth, descriptions are found repeatedly of fearsome energies, forces, entities, principalities and powers. The accounts often describe fierce battles of the will to overcome fear in meeting evil. Descriptions of the training of shamen and mystics emphasize the necessity of overcoming fear in these encounters. This is often the first important trial of the candidate for initiation. Interestingly, similar accounts abound in classical literature, as we read of a hero facing a fearsome and often supernatural foe. Time after time, the hero overcomes this enemy by virtue of his courage in facing it. Repeatedly, the stories describe a metamorphosis of the dragon or evil enemy at the point of climax when the hero finds an inner strength. The stories portray this finding of courage and inner serenity as the ultimate weapon.

And so it is.

The task of the Meta-Human is to take absolute control and responsibility for all aspects of his life. This is not done independently of the Source of Life but rather in alliance with God. Still, these legends repeat that even a person dedicated to divine purpose will meet this "trial of fear." Shouldn't an alliance with the good, the divine, preclude ever being faced with a fearsome, threatening enemy? Actually it should, and it can. We should notice that in classical mythology, the alliance with good does eventually overcome the foe but only after a particular action by our hero. It is this act that we are looking for to provide ultimate protection in our spiritual growth experience.

THE DRAGON OF PURITY

The action is an expression of utter confidence in our Source of protection. The expression of inner serenity comes from knowing your motivation to be "pure." Purity is another common feature of classical mythology. The purity required is not the purity of a virgin in a literal sense, but a purity of purpose. Purity of purpose means that our purpose is to be "whole," and not to gain power over others. Mystical courage arises from knowing we are protected. This knowledge of protection comes, in turn, from knowing the purity of purpose in encountering the opponent.

A PAGE FROM A BED-TIME STORY

The most profound mythology often appears in the guise of a children's story. The fable, the bedtime story and the fairy tale often symbolize the sacred texts of a Mystery School. Children sometimes experience "nightmares." A nightmare is an expression of anxiety. The monsters in a child's nightmare are not to be laughed at. They are the very real challenges of life that a growing, learning child must deal with. The monsters in a shamanic initiation are real in the same way. The monsters or threats that appear in altered states of consciousness are the embodiment of challenges not met in daily life. They appear in our meditations, dreams and nightmares to let us know that an unresolved challenge exists in our psyche.

When a child experiences a nightmare, there is a simple technique that may help overcome the fear. Tell the child that her finger has the power to "shrink a monster." Don't tell the child that pointing the finger will make the monster go away; it won't. But pointing the finger will almost certainly make the monster smaller. You have given the child a very real technique for encountering fear. She now has a means to cope with the monster/challenge. Does this mean that the child's anxiety (as personified by the monster) will go away? No. But it does mean that the child will reduce the threat and the power of the anxiety to a level she can cope with. You have given her something to do, a sense of personal power with which to face the anxiety symbolized by the monster. This simple act will extend to "shrink" the actual anxiety, even when neither you nor she knows what the anxiety is. This is not a false sense of security. It is, in fact, an affirmation of personal power over the challenges of life.

IS THIS A CHILD'S GAME?

When an adult begins to explore the recesses of the mind or spirit, she can uncover monsters and devils that are very real. People who have experimented with an ouija board or automatic writing very often contact fearsome "spirits" or energies. Hence the warnings to avoid such practices because they are "of the devil." That may be true. It will be true if there are "devils" lying unresolved in your "subconscious" or "unconscious" mind. Remember that I have said that the only danger that is greater than exploring these realms is the danger of not exploring them. If unresolved conflicts lie buried in your consciousness, it is a good idea to uncover them and "cast them out." Remember that I have also said that a good and experienced guide or teacher/counselor is essential to help you through these experiences of growth.

WHERE DO THE MONSTERS/DEVILS COME FROM?

A classic experience of people who "dabble" in occult matters may be described this way:

A person becomes intrigued with the idea of "spirit communication." He sets off on his own, or with a friend, and attempts such communication using the notorious ouija board or automatic writing. At first it is simply amusing when unexpected "messages" come. Then, it becomes more intriguing as the person wonders about the source of the messages. The messages tend to be "spiritual" or religious in nature and begin often with flattery. The writing will tell the participant that he/she is a "chosen vessel" for a very important work. These messages may continue. Then the messages take a turn. Now the source of the messages begins to admonish the experimenter for not being "pure" enough. Soon, the experimenter may be driven to an unreasonable period of fasting, praying and other exercises of "purification" or self-punishment. These experiences can sometimes extend threats to physical, mental and emotional health.

What happened? Are such demonic spirits real? Is possession really a possibility?

It is important to know that each of us has some measure of buried guilt. We also are likely to have a need to be "a chosen vessel" for divine purpose. This is often the real motivating factor for people who dabble in occult practices. These combined elements are a "set-up" for a frightening experience.

I do not wish to enter a theological argument on whether "devils" exist or whether "possession" is a valid phenomenon. Both can be experienced as sufficiently real to threaten health and sanity. This does not necessarily mean that there is a "kingdom of devils" in the sense that the animal kingdom and mankind exist. It does mean that a person with unresolved inner conflict and a need for self-importance as a spiritual "chosen vessel" is a poor candidate for attempting to "channel" or become a psychic. Entering a spiritual experiment for a sense of self importance violates the "purity of purpose" warning that precedes this section. Whether devils are real is, then, a rhetorical question. Whether a person should play with an ouija board or attempt automatic writing is not the relevant question. The relevant question to be considered is how to deal with buried guilt and the negative self-image that motivates one to need to be "a chosen vessel." If one is in any doubt about unresolved guilt or negative self-worth, there are better ways than an ouija board experiment to find out and resolve these questions. Certainly some form of therapy or counseling should precede any such attempts when there is a question.

HOW BETTER, THEN, TO PROCEED?

I have suggested that a concrete form of guidance (asking questions and getting clear answers) is one of the "mega-tools" of the Meta-Human. If not automatic writing and/or the ouija board, then how can one develop these "gifts?"

FIRST, ESTABLISH SELF-LOVE, SELF-WORTH, SELF-ESTEEM AND ALRIGHTNESS

The first step in establishing self-worth is self-forgiveness. We are all aware of 'miss-steps' in life. We have each violated our own principles at some time or other. Forgive yourself completely. Grant yourself the right to make mistakes and always forgive yourself when you do. Deal with the consequences of your mistakes when they affect the lives of others, if you can.

SELF-LOVE COMES FIRST

Love for self precedes even your love for your Source. The reason for this is that if you have not forgiven and appreciated your self, you will form a relationship with God that will agree with your negative self-assessment.

NOW LOVE GOD AND OTHERS

The Christ expressed the admonition, "Thou shalt love the Lord thy God with all thy might and love your neighbor as yourself." This was His statement of "the whole law." Notice that love for God and love for others is compared with your love for self. "As your self" is the key to learning how to love God and others.

BEGIN TO COMMUNICATE AND LISTEN

Make a practice of communication with the Source of your self every day. Talk to your Source even if you do not experience a clear answer or response. Continue your communication daily for forty days without missing a day. The forty day period will give you ample time to "get to know" the Source you are communicating with. A friendship will develop if you are comfortable with yourself. If you are loving your-self, you will expect love from your Source. This is the most favorable of circumstances for initiating a communication of guidance.

By the forty-first day, you will have begun to realize that answers have been coming, perhaps in subtle ways. Continue the process. Don't ever stop. Make this daily conversation a life-long pursuit. The answers will be clear enough in time. (Further instruction in this forty day process is found in Chapter 10.)

THE FEAR DRAGON STRIKES AGAIN

Even if I avoid such games as ouija boards and automatic writing, there may be fearful experiences in dreams or in meditation. What do I do when I experience fear? There are several teachers who suggest such simple techniques as "surround yourself with light" (whatever that means) or "ask for protection" (that is easy enough once you have established experiential contact with your Source). Some say, "Use a positive affirmation," or simply "Refuse to see it as evil, image it differently and it will go away."

While these instructions are meant well and are partly effective, they do not deal with important issues. One important issue is whether evil is real, or merely an illusion. In fact, anything real enough to cause harm is real enough. There is an argument that all matter is illusion. In any case, whatever we perceive, especially when threatening, is real enough to take seriously.

Then what do we do when faced with fear or with forces or entities that appear to be evil? How can we gain that required confidence and serenity to produce metamorphosis of the perceived threat?

MEET THE CHALLENGE IN ADVANCE

The challenge is one to be met well in advance. The moment of meeting a fearsome enemy is a late moment to gather weapons. The clarity, confidence and inner serenity needed for a moment of altered consciousness is also required for meeting the other challenges of life. If it is there as a habit, as a way of life, it will be there when the enemy is met. The confidence, courage, inner serenity and assurance of divine protection come from a right relationship with self and Source. When one who does not have a familiar and comfortable relationship with God calls upon Him in prayer, it is done so with fear and a lack of assurance. There will be a likelihood of feeling guilty and undeserving. These conditions will actually add to the fearsomeness of the enemy. Such simple techniques as "pray for protection," "visualize differently," or "surround yourself with light" are of no use to a person who feels inadequate, guilty or distant from Source.

THE DRAGON OF EGO

All the dragons are masters of disguise. It seems the ego dragon may be the cleverest of them all. There is a concerted effort by most of us to do battle with the dragon of self- importance. I have seen so many people belittle themselves and respond to the slightest hint of self-confidence with protest and fear. All but a few do a very admirable job of battling the dragon of over-confidence and self-importance. And so we should. Over- confidence, conceit and self-importance are enemies to balanced growth. But it is disguised. Conceit is not what it seems. One who feels alright is not conceited, not "better-than," but "alright." Over-confidence, conceit and self-importance are usually over- compensation devices for a person who does not, in fact, feel acceptable or alright. While we do battle with our fear that we may become conceited, we invite in a subtler dragon.

The subtler dragon of ego wears the label "humility," but that is not its name. Its name is "lack of appreciation for what I am." In over-reacting to the threat of ego, we too often despise and belittle self and undermine the confidence needed to do good work. The dragon of ego is conquered by developing a healthy ego that is a servant, not a master. It is an expression of balance that includes, at once, an appreciation for what I am and a humble (not self-deprecating) thankfulness for that.

THE OTHER FACE OF THE DRAGON OF EGO

Feeling inadequate can lead to the very great danger of seeking importance or acceptability by subordinating self to someone seen as more "spiritual" or acceptable. The inadequate or guilt-ridden person may enter a meditational state seeking a spirit-guide or master. This is a tendency that can actually lead to psychosis in a spiritual pursuit.

Instead of developing a healthy relationship with my creativity or "higher mind," I may feel that I must seek a spiritual master or guru to admire, worship or to depend upon to be what I believe I cannot. This can be a very grave mistake. Keep in mind that to worship and pay homage to someone who has made great spiritual advancement reinforces my lack. The very act of worshiping another may become a substitute for accomplishing what I admire in this person's accomplishments. Is not the goal to be that, rather than admire it?

Certainly, there is great advantage to knowing an accomplished Meta-Human. In fact, admiration of such a person or teacher is appropriate. We may even serve this person's needs to receive such insight as we can from the experience. Certainly, I would do this, and have. If I expect great insight from a teacher, there is not enough that I can do to serve in such a way as to make it possible for her/him to have more time to share with me and others who learn from his experience. This is quite different from worshiping and expecting a substitute for my alrightness. No valid teacher will allow such worship. Neither will a spirit or spirit guide emphasize greatness or holiness as compared to your unworthiness.

Any teacher who emphasizes personal "status" or greatness is to be avoided. Great teachers are servants, and if they allow themselves to be served, it is to make their time more available to those who "think they are serving" while, in reality, it is the student who is being served. A teacher may allow a student to serve, for the purpose of learning to serve as the teacher is serving.

ANOTHER DRAGON WAITS HERE

The following scenario is all too common among those who seek to become "psychic" rather than becoming whole. A guilty,inadequate person entertains a fantasy of becoming a "psychic channel." He or she believes that by giving "readings" or communications from "spirit" or "spirits," importance and acceptability will result. In this dangerous state of mind, and for ego purposes, he or she will meditate and see or hear communications that often tell others what to do. Soon other "inade-quate" people are flocking for "guidance." These are people who never graduated from the child-state in which all decisions were made by mommy and daddy. Those who follow after psychics are often those who need parent substitutes to relieve responsibility for decision-making.

Does this mean one should never visit a psychic or spiritual coun-selor? Actually, everyone who seeks pastoral guidance is consulting a psychic. Virtually all ministers purport to draw on divine guidance in counseling. They are, then, to some extent, channeling information from spiritual sources in counseling. Certainly, intuitive counseling or even inspired readings can be very helpful. The person who never seeks another's point of view is a fool. But so are those who allow others to make decisions for them.

There are those who show great talent in channeling guidance and spiritual help for others. Reliable guidance, however, should be aimed at making situations clearer so that intelligent decisions can be made. The gifted spiritual counselor or psychic will not tell others what to do but will help to illuminate possibilities.

The same scenario often results in the compounding of problems. The budding psychic started with a sense of guilt and feelings of inade-quacy. After beginning to "receive messages," something may be done for which guilt is felt. It may be something quite unrelated to "channeling." Now with this guilt, the person returns to meditate again. Naturally, his or her spirit source is very holy and disapproving of the mistake. The communication may be a scolding. Indeed, the budding psychic may have to fantasize punishment from "source" to maintain its quality in his mind. I have seen such sad experiences lead into a feeling of being controlled by the "spirit" who becomes very abusive.

These dangerous situations are the results of two dangerous misconceptions:

> 1. That I need something, or someone, outside of self to give guidance to me and make decisions for me.

> 2. That I am unworthy and inadequate.

The development of character is most important before attempting these things.

Seeking guidance of the Source is not a matter of contacting someone else. Simply stated, God in me is a quality of life who can come to life in me, not someone else who can talk to me. The development of God-consciousness is the perfection of what God made my mind to be. It is the experience of discovering the potential within and allowing the "God-part" within me to become the decision-making factor.

THE DRAGON OF POWER

All the dragons are one, thus the overcoming of the dragons will return to essentially one theme - overcoming fear with love. The need for power is a love substitute. If I feel loved, I will not have a lust for power over others or a need to prove that I am powerful. If I am alright, I will not need power to prove it.

This temptation is perhaps the most common enemy of the very promising Meta-Human. The first taste of power, the first experience of being able to do what others cannot, is exceptionally demanding upon strength of character. A person with strength of character is usually thought to possess the qualities of honesty and humility and to have high moral standards. Certainly these are indications of strength of character but they are results, not causes. One does not become honest and humble and develop high moral standards in order to build strength of character. Strength of character instead produces those results. Too often, humans have made great effort to achieve the results while not considering that there is a very basic cause that automatically produces such results.

Stated simply, the basis for strong character is an elusive quality called "alrightness." It is the consistent experience of feeling loved, acceptable and accepted. Absolute honesty is a result of no need to appear other than as I am. It does not come from trying to be honest. Honesty is a result of the lack of any need to be dishonest. True humility is a result of knowing who and what I am with no need for comparison with others. High moral standards are a result of being fulfilled. The ill-defined need for satisfactions is filled by constant assurance of being loved. Experiencing constant joy replaces any need for perverse entertainment or substitute attempts at satisfaction.

THE DRAGON OF GUILT

No one is so vulnerable as the guilty. This dragon is especially powerful because each of us has a very active memory of some act we can easily feel guilty about. These memories are so available and sometimes so powerful that just when we are beginning to feel good about our relationship with self and Source, the guilt dragon pops up to show that ugly head.

Guilt is an important tool to the person who is serious about growth and change. The purpose of guilt is to make us aware of a mistake or failure. It is important to recognize mistakes. Guilt is an important tool for impressing upon us the significance of error. For this reason, guilt should be appreciated, even welcomed as an asset. Then, having done the job, the servant should be dismissed. Too often, we feel a need to be punished for our mistake or failure. Then we may assign our servant, "Guilt," the task of beating us over the head with a reminder of failure as if to purge ourselves. There is a perverse feeling that if we feel guilty enough, long enough, we are made better. We may have a belief that this is necessary to be forgiven. Whether from a psychological or a religious point of view, this is not so.

Psychologically, guilt is incapacitating and increases the likelihood of repeating the same error because it reinforces our belief in vulnerability to such error. Religiously, the instruction is to "confess."

Confession is a clear acknowledgement of a thought or activity that is not in harmony with the person I want to be. This acknowledgement must not include any excuse, explanation or justification. Acknowledgement without justification indicates acceptance of responsibility. "Responsible" could well be thought of as "response-able." The very fact that I feel guilty is an indication that I am can to respond and that the desire to do better is active and alive. That is enough! Guilt has done its job. The servant has reminded you that the motivation to grow and to be effective is alive and well within you. It is cause for joy and congratulations, not for punishment and beating self. The Bible says it well: "Repent (change direction) and I will separate your sin from you as far as the east is from the west and remember it no more."[1]

The Source that you apologize to is so willing to forget your error that taking a new direction erases the record of it. I have an image of God being delighted to forget a mistake and get on with the growth process. The guilty person keeps bringing up the memory of the error until God says, "Enough! I have already forgiven that, so quit bringing it up! I'm tired of your waving the ugly thing before my face." (I apologize for personifying God in such childlike terms, but the imagery serves well.) Again the Bible states, "If we confess (state clearly) our errors, He is absolutely dependable to both forgive and remove the tendency to so err."[2]

The removal of the tendency to so err is not possible while I keep it alive through restating my guilt. It is even valuable to recognize that each time I bring up my guilt. It is like committing the error again because I have given it new life and new power to affect me.

Don't just ask forgiveness, forgive yourself. It is not possible for your Source to forgive you when you keep your guilt alive by not forgiving self. The communication of forgiveness from your Source cannot be heard above your own self accusation. Accept the Biblical promise as fact. If you have acknowledged it, it is forgiven. Take that for granted and get on with it, however terrible the act. It is forgotten. No valid purpose is served by reminding yourself of failure. In fact, if the act is so terrible, that is all the more reason not to add to its influence by giving it continuing power over you.

THE DRAGONS OF THE SUBCONSCIOUS

It is a rare person, indeed, who grows to maturity without storing unresolved conflicts and stresses in the subconscious. In our early years we tend to personify these conflicts as monsters, the stuff of nightmares. It is natural to think in symbols especially during childhood. Monsters and unresolved stresses and fears of the day haunt our dreams as nightmare animals. Any serious growth effort will unlock the closets of the subconscious. When we begin to relax and get to know self better, we often need to clean these closets and resolve the stored fears and stresses that "pop up" in frightening images or disturbing feelings. There is a need for a harmonious relationship with the subconscious. It is here that belief systems are stored. These beliefs are the basis for emotions and habits. We often hold beliefs that we do not recognize. Upon examination many of them are easily recognized as irrational, and merely becoming aware of them may liberate us from their tyranny. There are safe techniques for releasing these stored stresses and for making friends with the subconscious.

PANDORA'S BOX

The great teachers have often warned that the pursuit of growth is like the opening of Pandora's box. We may be tempted to leave the lid on and sit on it. These dragons may seem overwhelming. The important thing to recognize is that they exist and we will interact with them either intentionally (through deliberate growth) or unintentionally while trying to deny them. To avoid growth is to avoid life.

Remember, the first step in becoming the Meta-Human is the development of an inner serenity that is a result of a right relationship with self and Source. This is the foundation for character building and the foundation for effectiveness.

CHAPTER VIII

Becoming Meta-Human; Relationship With Self

*"The need to obtain alrightness from others
is a result of an irrational belief system
and is 'learned.'"*

The greatest mistakes in growth come from a lack of what we will call "alrightness." It is this quality that we will seek to establish and maintain throughout our study. Factually, you have it already. It is yours. You were born with it. It is a birthright. But the facts don't matter if you fail to recognize or believe them. The seeking of alrightness is the single greatest motivating force known to man. Almost everything you do is oriented toward establishing or proving alrightness. The fear of not having alrightness can cause you to take foolish action that is not in your own best interest. It is very likely that you have already experienced this in your relationships and communications.

You decorate your home to communicate alrightness. You dress to communicate alrightness. You may have studied grammar and diction to prove alrightness. You likely choose your friends, join certain groups and go to the "right" places to communicate or establish alrightness.

You may have lied to yourself about some of these things. You may think that you decorated your house for your own comfort. How many things you bought would be there if you knew nobody else would ever see them? How much money would you save if you spent no money buying alrightness?

I am not condemning the practice of surrounding yourself with beautiful things, or even the practice of communicating your alrightness. I am merely suggesting that you should be aware of your motivation and be honest with yourself. I am also suggesting that you remove

---

Please forgive our creative spelling of "alright," rather than the proper "all right." We are coining the term "alrightness" with appropriate definition.

anxiety that the need for alrightness can produce. Then take responsibility for your own alrightness.

WHERE DOES THE NEED FOR ALRIGHTNESS COME FROM?

This incredible drive to establish and communicate alrightness is not natural or inherent. It is a phenomenon of our irrational culture.

You and I were born into an irrational culture. We were taught many beliefs, values and habits that are not rational. Many beliefs and practices we take for granted and think of as inherent and universal are cultural phenomena. Interestingly, many of the beliefs are proven invalid upon the slightest examination. Many of the values are quite easily proven worthless. Yet, they are perpetuated from generation to generation and, unfortunately, often cause pain and dis-ease.

One of the most common irrational beliefs is that someone else can give me my "alrightness." Many people spend their whole lives building a career, making money, and impressing people to gain alrightness. It is the drive that creates politicians, makes people run for president, motivates entertainers. With sufficient drive (or hunger), one might "reach the top." Unfortunately, it may be then that he or she realizes that it didn't work. Certainly it is good to know that "Many people voted for him" (a statement of alrightness) or "She accumulated many fans and received praise," but it doesn't work. Any number of people can communicate their opinion that I am alright, but if I haven't discovered that for myself, I will not believe them.

Perhaps the Presidency is the ultimate example of this irrational belief system. Every four years, several people with a terribly exaggerated need to be assured of alrightness spend a fortune and endure absurd abuse to satisfy their great hunger. Several receive a communication that they are not alright. One receives a temporary assurance of alrightness, then is put in a position of being told, "You are not alright," for at least four years. This one may then spend the next several years after leaving office, trying to justify personal alrightness by writing self-defense memoirs or sadly go away to die. Maybe this cynicism is overstated. I only wish there were not an ounce of truth in it.

Although the highest office in our country is the ultimate example of this drive for alrightness, those people not interested in the Presidency are certainly not immune to the hunger. We teach our children in the earliest grades in school to seek alrightness. It is the most basic drive we teach. Making high marks is not so much a matter of learning as it is receiving alrightness from someone else.

Those who do not receive alrightness from others are punished twice. Failure to receive recognition is the first punishment. Then the "failures" are punished again for the failure. This, of course, is the classic source of the criminal and antisocial element. The failures will now seek a substitute. Refused a statement of alrightness, they will seek other forms of attention. A basic survival need is being deprived and survival demands a substitute.

The list of substitutes for alrightness is horrifying. Men and women will settle for sympathy, hate, punishment, condemnation, fear, power, money, sex and the fulfillment of other appetites. Just as receiving statements of alrightness from others is unsatisfying, so, too, all these substitutes leave an insatiable hunger.

THE FIVE BASIC SURVIVAL NEEDS

You have several basic survival needs. Some of these are obvious. You need food. You need water. You need air to breathe, sunlight and shelter. These needs are obvious enough to be taken for granted. It is not difficult to admit these needs. To have such needs is not considered a sign of weakness. They are so obvious and so universal that no one would criticize your admitting such needs. But there is another survival need that is not so easy to admit. In fact, to speak of a need is often considered a sign of weakness.

THE SIXTH SURVIVAL NEED

The sixth survival need is often called the need for approval, attention or alrightness. It is more accurately the need for love. Some years ago it was discovered that institutionalized babies often die even though the five basic survival needs were met. They suffered from what was termed "institutional illness." It was soon established that a sixth basic survival need was not being met. The need was for consistent personal attention and care. A need for love.

LOVE AS AN ENERGY OF LIFE

There is no denying that everyone has emotional needs. Emotion plays an important part in our well-being and self-expression. Emotion can, in fact, cause physical changes. But did babies really die as a result of the failure to have their emotional needs met? While that is possible, it is more likely that there is an actual energy exchange involved in the process we call love. There is interesting evidence that this is so.

A few years ago, I was approached by a science writer. He was studying the results of experiments performed in the Soviet Union. According to his account, Soviet scientists had connected a mother rabbit to bio-feedback equipment while her babies were systematically killed. Each time a baby rabbit died, she registered a reaction on the equipment. The babies had been shielded from her presence so that she could not react through ordinary sensory channels. In an attempt to identify the nature of the energy that evidently traveled from baby rabbit to mother rabbit, the experiment was extended. To test for magnetism or electricity as a conductor and to introduce time and space as factors, the baby rabbits were taken beneath the ocean in a submarine about 500 miles from the location of the mother rabbit. Lead shields and other inhibiting factors were introduced. The mother rabbit still reacted every time a baby rabbit was killed, and there was no apparent time lapse between their death and her reaction in spite of the distance. There is no known energy that can overcome these barriers of time, space and matter, yet something was obviously traveling a great distance. And it was apparently delivering an intelligible message or was having a physical effect! The writer requested that I consult my Source of intuitive guidance and ask about the nature of this energy. In an altered state of consciousness, I asked and waited. The answer came:

"To coin a term, the energy is 'Logoidal energy,' this Source of thought explained, referring to the Gospel of John. "In the beginning was the Logos (or expression) of God. Everything that was made was made by, and out of, that expression. The creative energy, the basic or prime energy of the universe is the energy of the Logos, the energy of God expressing Himself."

Another Biblical statement declares, "God is Love." The creative or Logoidal (or logoic) energy is the energy called love. It is the energy of cell building and repair, the greatest energy in the universe. Because all matter is made from it, no matter inhibits its transference. It is a vital energy, necessary for survival.

According to this communication, something we have often thought of as an emotion is a vital and important energy capable of affecting matter.

THERAPEUTIC TOUCH

Another interesting experiment at New York University may confirm this concept of energy transfer. Dr. Delores Krieger, a professor of nursing, established experiments in "laying-on-of-hands" healing, or "therapeutic touch." Using groups of nurses in control groups, she found evidence that a healing touch can change the hemoglobin count and elevate the amount of oxygen in the blood. Both are indicators of a healing process at work. She found that it did not work every time. She began to eliminate variables. She tested to see if religious nurses could do it better. They could not. She tested to see if nurses who "believed in it" could do it better. They could not. Eliminating several other variables, she finally tested to see whether nurses were more effective when they cared particularly about a specific patient. This element of caring proved to be the variable she was looking for. It gave consistent results. The X-factor in "laying-on-of-hands" healing was love!

There are, in fact, several other indicators of the importance of this factor in health and well-being. A patient who loves self and life will heal faster. A patient who despises a part of the body (perhaps the genitals or even the feet) will deny healing to that specific portion. A patient who feels loved by the physician will respond and "get well for the doctor."

Clearly love is an important, even vital, perhaps essential, factor in survival and well-being. But what is love? Any attempt to define this energy/emotion seems inadequate. In fact, it becomes all the more confusing when you consider how many people depend on alternate forms of attention we would not ordinarily characterize as love. What do sympathy, disapproval, punishment and even hate have in common with love? The common factor is that they all communicate caring. I cannot hate you unless I care. I would not have the energy to actively hate you if you did not matter to me. And so it is with the other love substitutes. The fact is, these substitutes are variations of love, of what might be called misguided or distorted love, but love none the less. And we will settle for them if we cannot obtain a healthy form of love. We seem to be saying, "If I can cause you to react, then I matter." We gain a form of alrightness.

The love substitutes, or alrightness substitutes, are often gained by anti-social actions or actions not in my own best interest. Even worse, the attention I receive is not satisfying and requires repetition or even escalation in an attempt to "scratch the itch."

The problem is prevalent in our society. Who is there who has not used one or more of the substitutes to gain attention? How many of us have grown whole enough to never use them now?

A UNIVERSAL NEED OR A LEARNED NEED?

The need for alrightness is natural and inherent. You and I were born with "alrightness." We are inherently alright. Being alright, AND

KNOWING IT is a universal need. However, the need to obtain alright-ness FROM OTHERS is a result of an irrational belief system and is "learned."

There are, in fact, two irrationalities in the belief system. It is irrational to consider that I am not alright. It is further irrational to assume that if I am not alright then I can become alright by getting others to communicate that I am alright.

WHAT IS ALRIGHTNESS?
HOW CAN I KNOW THAT I AM ALRIGHT?

Let's consider some facts about you. Keep in mind that these are facts, not suppositions. They are about you, personally. These facts are true about your body, about your mind and about your identity. They are true of the totality of you.

First use your body as an example. Your body is an intricate, delicate, complex and fascinating instrument. This is not even dependent on whether you are healthy. Your body is intricate, delicate, complex, fascinating and responsive. In fact, it is absolutely wonderful!

Imagine a highly trained computer technician called to diagnose and repair a malfunction, finding an instrument that is incredibly intricate. The intricacy of design alone is stunning to the impressed technician. The next discovery is that it is delicate and highly responsive. Now highly trained professional is amazed with the expertise of the designer and builder of such an amazing instrument. In the diagnostic search, it is finally discovered! The most amazing and wonderful fact of all, is that the fantastic instrument is not malfunctioning at all; it is simply doing exactly what it was designed to do. It is following precisely the programming tape entered into it. It is producing results precisely appropriate to a pre-programmed cause. Now, the challenge is to retrain the programmer or to correct the information used in the programming.

Your body is amazingly complex. More complex than the most sophisticated computer and much more efficient. It can do more things and it is more responsive than any computer. Your body is so responsive that it is impossible for you to think a thought, or experience an emotion that does not affect it. It is even self-repairing, given the right materials. It can correct the damage of an inappropriate thought, action or even material damage, repeatedly, and often return to full efficiency.

No matter what condition your body is in, it is still an intricate, delicate, complex, sophisticated, fascinating, wonderful and highly responsive instrument. It is fantastic!

Your mind is all this as well. It is responsive and wonderful. It is creative and effective. It does use beliefs as programming material and those beliefs may often be wrong, even irrational. But it is often capable of correcting the results of wrong thought, belief and action — even producing physical results.

What you are is wonderful. You are fascinating. You could fascinate the most inquisitive scientist or researcher for an age or more. You are fascinating to people around you. You are wonderful and there are no exceptions to these facts.

We try to find our alrightness through our accomplishments but you are more than alright, even without accomplishments. The value of your accomplishment is the value of what you have done. Your value is in what you are. You are alright.

We may try to find alrightness in accumulation of possessions. Their value is in them. You are not alright because you have or can obtain. You are alright.

Your alrightness has a need. It can be a balancing, healthy force but it must be fed. It must be validated, recognized. But there is only one validation or recognition that will work. You cannot receive validation of your alrightness from me. I can recognize your alrightness. I can assure you of it. I can give my recognition, but you will invalidate it if you have not recognized it yourself. Only you can affirm your alrightness and you do not need permission. You do not need agreement. You are the authority. No one else is qualified to judge.

In a religious sense, you could say that God has given you a wonderful, intricate, delicate instrument. Failure to recognize that is surely an insult to your creator.

BUT WHAT ABOUT HUMILITY?

There are two kinds of humility. There is a constructive humility that will work for you, and there is a destructive humility that will work against you. The destructive humility says, "Who me? Oh, I'm not so much." That is very much like a craftsman who has a great job to do but is denying the value of his tools. The only gain is an excuse to not do a good job. It is an insult to your Source. Constructive humility says, "I realize that what I am is wonderful, and I am thankful for that. Having such fascinating attributes must be a great responsibility. I accept that responsibility." Constructive humility is a deep sense of appreciation and responsibility.

You were given a body, a mind and an identity, all of which require

71

love to survive. You are responsible for meeting all your survival needs. You are responsible for meeting all the needs of your body, mind and self. They all need love; it is literally a survival need. To make others responsible for your personal needs is to be irresponsible. Others cannot meet that need. Your body and your mind are your children. They must have your love, approval and appreciation. Without it these wonderful instruments will malfunction; but even then, they will be wonderful instruments, deserving of your love and appreciation.

CHAPTER IX

Learning To Love Yourself

"As long as self-deprecation is a badge of humility
and spirituality, we will continue to produce
emotional cripples in spiritual growth."

LEARNING TO LOVE YOURSELF

To say that we can love others, but not self, is not likely to be true. To love others is to give others a very worthwhile energy. It has great value. If I know that my love is worthwhile and has great value, then I must have appreciation for my love and for myself as a giver of love. Appreciation of the value of my love implies some love for myself. If what I am giving others is something I feel is of little value, it must not be love. It is more likely that I am giving others a sort of kindness and appreciation aimed at gaining something in return. This is a selfish motivation and can hardly be called love.

Love is a survival need. We must have it to survive. Survival is our own responsibility. Acceptance of responsibility is the hallmark of the Meta-Human. Responsibility becomes response- ability. Response-ability is the ability to respond appropriately to the challenges of life. The first responsibility is responsibility for self. If we are not accepting total responsibility for self, we are giving away our power over self and living in victim consciousness. Providing the love we need for survival is a primary responsibility. Learning to love self comes first through acceptance of responsibility. See it as a responsibility, not a luxury. It is not "just nice" to be able to love self. It is a responsibility. Recognizing that may make it easier to learn self-love.

WHY WE BELIEVE IT IS DIFFICULT

We have been taught to believe that self love is selfish. We are also taught that "saints" are selfless. If our goal is spiritual growth, we may be highly motivated to become selfless.

HERE IS A PARADOX

The great Wisdom Schools are also called "Mystery Schools." These schools teach "The Greater and the Lesser Mysteries." The mysteries are called mysteries because they are often stated in paradox (also called "chohans"). Resolving the paradox or chohan is the revealing of a mystery. The apparent paradox of selflessness is that it requires self love. When you have sufficient self love, you will be free to love others without thinking of self first. That is the resolution of the paradox or mystery of unconditional love.

YOU ARE SUPPOSED TO TRY, BUT NOT SUCCEED

Perhaps the most important barrier to self-love is our cultural belief system. While psychologists and teachers, spiritual leaders and almost everyone is emphasizing the importance of self- love these days, there remains a persistent belief that it is better to "try to love myself" than to really accomplish it. In fact, "I'm trying to learn to love myself" is a statement made in a self-serving, almost boastful way at most seminars and self-improvement workshops. It sounds a little dishonest, doesn't it? The real communication is, "I want you to know that I am too humble and indeed, too spiritually advanced to accomplish self-love." Clearly, we haven't all believed yet that it is alright to succeed at self-love. As long as self-deprecation is a badge of humility and spirituality, we will continue to produce emotional cripples in spiritual growth. The message needs to become clear that to despise yourself is to exhibit a gross lack of appreciation for your Source. It is to accuse our Creator of inadequacy and ineffectiveness. How can a person who so doubts the effectiveness of God be spiritual?

MISDIRECTING LOVE

There is another misperception often at fault in our difficulty with self-love. It is the tendency to equate what we are with what we have done. How can I love myself when I am so aware of my faults?

It is not important to love your faults, nor do you need to love yourself because of your successes. Despising your faults may be a part of loving yourself, but despising your faults is quite different from blaming yourself for having faults. It is alright to make mistakes. Think of yourself as "your child."

IT IS EASIER TO LOVE A CHILD

Children often make mistakes. It is a part of growing up. Children may even deliberately do unkind things. As parents, we may deeply disapprove. We would be ineffective parents if we did not, but we do not disapprove of the child. How often we have seen a proud father, even while a child is misbehaving, boast, "That's my boy." It is alright to make mistakes. How often we find it easy to forgive others what we condemn in ourselves. We may hear someone feeling guilty and miserable for some failure and find it easy to say,"That's alright, don't be so hard on yourself." We may even see how ridiculous it is to be so guilt-ridden. Why not try forgiving and supporting yourself as you forgive and support others when they make mistakes?

A DEFINITION OF LOVE

There have been many attempts to define love. Most are woefully inadequate. It is somehow related to attraction to others, appreciation for others, support or even a chemical reaction. It has something to do with being kind, sympathetic and understanding. It is something that cements relationships. But what is it?

It may be that the Bible has the best answer. "God is Love," says John. God is love and love has an opposite. The opposite of love is not hate. You cannot hate someone unless you care. You will not have the energy to hate someone who doesn't matter. Hate is misguided love. The true opposite of love is fear.If the terms God and love are synonymous, so fear and evil are synonymous. Fear is defined as faith in evil. Love is faith in good. Self-love is having faith in the good in me. Loving others is expressing faith in them.

THE THREE TWO-FOLD ASPECTS OF LOVE

Each Aspect Has Two Facets

I. KINDNESS/CARING

Kindness is action which results from caring.

Kindness is the action of love. Kindness characterizes all actions that come from love.

Caring is a state of being which results from recognition of value.

Caring is not a communication, but it does communicate. What caring communicates is that the object of my caring matters to me.

2. UNDERSTANDING/ACCEPTANCE

Understanding may be the most sought after facet of love. We are willing to go to incredible lengths to be understood. The "hallmark" of a good counselor, for example, is the wisdom to hear and appreciate just how deep, serious and insurmountable a problem is before offering a solution. In fact, caring persons often discover that when a distraught person feels understood, the problem "magically" diminishes, power is released and the anguished person discovers or reveals the sought after answer or solution.

It must be noted that understanding is not intellectual. It is not arrived at by logic, but rather by empathy. Understanding results from "a willingness to understand."

Acceptance denotes the unconditional quality of love. The term "unconditional love" is redundant because that which is conditional is not love. While we may place conditions upon our rewards for another's action or response and still maintain an underlying love, it is not the love that is conditional. Where love is real, a person may disappoint us and we may withhold reward, but our love clings tenaciously to our relationship.

The acceptance facet of love communicates, "I accept you exactly as you are without any requirement that you change to meet my expectations.

Acceptance is such a vital facet of love that we may indulge in unacceptable behavior in relationships to "test" whether another person really loves us or whether the love is strong enough to endure. We may then refuse to change unacceptable behavior until we are accepted and loved in spite of it. This "testing" for unconditional love is often the basis for misbehavior in children and may be the most important key to understanding criminal behavior in adults.

3. CHALLENGE/SERVICE

The third aspect of love may be called challenge/service and may be the trickiest challenge in the development of "the perfect love which casts out fear." The challenge aspect of love refers to the ability to encourage a loved one to grow and to express her highest potential without resorting to the destructive and undermining tactics of criticism and disapproval. The "tricky" part is to communicate encouragement to express highest potential without implying a lack of acceptance of the person as they are. Even more tricky is the possibility that the person you believe in and encourage may harbor feelings of guilt and inadequacy and may feel that your confidence is misplaced. They may even feel "phony" at having "misled you" and develop a need to prove to you that they are not so wonderful as you thought and are incapable of meeting your expectations.

If the challenge aspect of love involves such pitfalls, how can we successfully avoid them?

Remember that love, though it has at least three aspects, is one whole. If kindness, caring, understanding and acceptance are alive in the relationship, you may exercise the challenge/service aspect of love without fear.

Service expresses the selfless quality of love. The important "control factor" to make service effective and real is to remember that weakness does not serve. Only strong, confident and fulfilled people serve well because they serve by choice, not out of necessity. Service is not self-deprecating. It may be self-effacing. Self-denial is not an essential to service but the master-servant finds self-denial a readily available option. One who is fulfilled has little need for calling attention to self. Those who adopt a placating, servile attitude in relationships are neither loving nor serving, they are rather battering their soul in the hope of pleasing another. The lack of self-acceptance creates a "soul poverty" of essential love and the self-victimized person batters self in the hope that another (or others) will accept responsibility for giving the acceptance, attention or alrightness necessary to survival. Werner Erhardt says in his Erhardt Seminars Training (EST), "You cannot help people, you can assist them." This distinction may clarify the nature of service and may assist in avoiding pitfalls.

Where these three two-fold aspects exist, there is love. If any one of the six facets is missing, love is incomplete.

CHAPTER X

Exercises In Building Self-Love

*"Absolutely everything that happens can and will serve
the interests of my life and experience."*

EXERCISE #1: THE TRUTH SHALL SET YOU FREE

Notice the conversation that goes on within your mind. Your internal conversation continues throughout your day and even during sleep. It does not always involve words; you use images, ideas and concepts to think conversations with yourself.

You also may notice that the conversation involves two "sides" of yourself. While there may be dozens of aspects of yourself, they all belong on one side or another of your inner conversation. I describe these two "sides" of yourself in the following ways.

THE ADVENTUROUS CHILD

There is a part of you that wants to do things. In its purest state this side of yourself is like an adventurous, perhaps unruly child who wants to rush out into the world and do, see, touch, feel, and experience absolutely everything. By nature, this innocent, naive child is a bit of a show-off and would like to make great speeches and act big, dramatic parts, or conduct orchestras. The child likes to stare at people and touch them. The adventurous child loves easily, is hurt easily, is vulnerable and must be protected.

THE GOVERNOR

Fortunately there is a rational, protective, inhibiting governor side of yourself. This inner parent learns early the necessity of bridling enthusiasm and stifling the adventurous child.

Depending upon your parent/teacher/adult and peer responses, the governor may have learned to use some very destructive techniques in managing the adventurous child.

The two sides of your self share one need in common. It is the need for the three facets of love (a need to be alright).

It appears that the adventurous child is inherent, and that the governor is learned or acquired while growing up and creating a personality.

You may believe what is said by others and become very cooperative, controlled and well-behaved (seeking approval). Or, you may be rebellious, renegade and seek attention (seek to be right and make others wrong) by misbehaving and resisting convention. One or both sides of self may choose to be confused and helpless, seeking a love substitute through being served and cared for by others.

One side may dominate. If the adventurous child is dominant, the result will likely be a playful, adventurous, free spirit who appears irresponsible. If the governor dominates, you are likely to be uptight, inhibited, and perhaps very proper or you may be painfully shy and fearful.

In any case, both exist. You will never completely squelch the child in you, though men, in particular, are encouraged to try.

IDENTIFYING THE TWO SIDES OF SELF

Notice your impulse (however squelched or latent) upon meeting new people. It may even be expressed in a hope that they will approach you so that you will not have to approach them.

Notice the "you" that would like to be different than you are. The "you" that would like to do things you would not really consider doing. That "you" that wanted to make good grades, see things, do things, accomplish things. The "you" that wonders (however fleetingly) what it would be like to be on stage acting a part or directing the affairs of some great concern. Notice the "you" that can hurt when others reject you and may even sometimes want to cry or to stamp your feet and be a bit childish.

The little child is sometimes seen clearly in the big, macho football player who slams the ball to the ground in frustration and may even fall face down to beat on the ground with his fists. What greater evidence of the little boy who still exists, who desperately wants to succeed and to be loved and appreciated. These qualities are "the adventurous child."

Now notice "the responsible adult self" who reasons that you should think twice before you do anything daring. Listen to that warning that you might be laughed at, that you would make a fool of yourself if you got up on stage, that you could never run the affairs of some big concern. This is the "you" who forbids you to cry when you're hurt because men don't cry and makes you act sheepish when you have just slammed the football to the ground in frustration. This is the "you" that noticed that other people were looking when you did that, and proceeded to tell you what they were probably thinking.

It is not necessary to distinguish clearly the two sides of self. They may even seem to "swap roles" occasionally. While this should not be taken too literally, the adventurous child is usually identified as "the intrinsic self" or "the inherent self." This implies that the child is "who you really are."

In her book titled **Talking to Yourself,** Dr. Pamela Butler speaks of "the intrinsic self" and "the imposed self." According to her hypothesis, the intrinsic self is the original "you." The imposed self is the "parental" or "judgmental" you that is a collection of the values of adult caretakers. This imposed self is the self that keeps you "in check," controlling your behavior according to society's rules and values.

I prefer to call the inner child your "inherent" self, because I believe that the "intrinsic" self is "God in you" or "the Inner Self Helper." The governor or parent is often described as "the imposed self," seemingly built from values of adult caretakers in your formative period.

GIVE EACH SIDE OF YOURSELF A NAME

If you now have a "feel" for the two sides of yourself, give each a name. I use my first name, Paul, to refer to the adult/governor and my middle name, Ben, for the child self.

Paul and Ben express "sibling rivalry" in several ways. If Ben should stumble on a crack in the sidewalk, Paul immediately exclaims, "Clumsy fool, why don't you stay conscious and watch where we're going?" Ben looks quickly to see if people are watching and turns red in the face but Paul immediately instructs him, "Keep your head up, don't look at the people who are watching. Pretend it didn't happen." Or Paul may say with an exaggerated look of disapproval, "Why can't they maintain these sidewalks?"

Ben and Paul may carry on a sullen and argumentative mood for several minutes and deprive themselves (self) of the available joy, laughter and beauty around them. Paul may even blame the light-hearted mood "we" were in for not noticing the sidewalk and could even direct a depressing mumble about how "these things 'always' happen just when I'm in a good mood. Something always happens to destroy it." He may even launch into a tirade about how bad the world is, how shoddy workmanship is these days and how no one cares any-more. Amazing how the seeds of depression can be planted by the self-talk resulting from a little incident.

THE CHALLENGE OF SELF-LOVE

The challenge is to get Paul (the governor/parent) and Ben (the adventurer/child) to love one another.

PROTECTING THE ADVENTUROUS CHILD

Paul is afraid to accept Ben just as he is. The fear is, "If I accept and approve of him just as he is, he won't get any better." Paul thinks, "I have an obligation to point out Ben's mistakes, his faults and limitations. I have to protect him, motivate him and control him. Without me, he would go wild, become egotistical and self-centered. He might make a fool of himself. After all, "I'm the voice of his conscience. I have to be blaming and scolding, it's my nature. Besides, I know all the things he's done wrong and how bad he's been. How can I possibly approve of him as he is? I'll give him love when he's good and I'll give him approval when he's successful. If I don't withhold love and approval now, he'll never be a success."

The reason Paul doesn't love Ben is fear. He is afraid to give him the three aspects of love.

THE CHILD FEARS THE GOVERNOR

Ben is afraid of Paul. Ben wants everything he sees if it is shining and appealing, but Paul says it is wrong to want things so Ben tries not to want. Ben wants to do everything, explore and be everything, but Paul says he can't. "You have to be realistic," says Paul. "Accept your limitations. And for goodness sake, keep quiet. Don't say everything that comes into your mind. People will think you're crazy."

Ben feels compared with others and feels inadequate. Even when he has successes, Paul assures him it is not enough. Ben believes Paul — most of the time. But there is an underlying belief in himself as well. "I'm not really as dumb as Paul says I am. I could be really smart if I wanted to. Maybe I'll really be a success one day."

But Ben is afraid to not believe Paul. Everyone else seems to agree with his values.

BORN OF FEAR

The truth is, of course, that Paul really does love Ben. He is devoted to him. But when he uses the tactics described above, it is misguided love. This is the result of "believing in fear."

And Ben loves Paul, but his respect for Paul and his belief in Paul as his salvation are both born of fear.

BELIEVING IN FEAR

Only two primary powers exist. These are commonly called, "Good and evil, right and wrong, life and death," or (my preference) "love and fear." The force of love and life empower everything that is encouraging, life-giving, effective and growth-producing. The force of fear and death empowers all that is discouraging, limiting and destructive.

Unfortunately, we have been taught to believe in fear. Our whole system of punishment, threats and warnings is based on a belief that fear will make us better, will protect us and will make us wise.

Nothing could be further from the truth. Since we believe that fear will make us better, Paul will continue to accuse, punish and belittle Ben, even when Ben is materially successful. Recent studies at the University of Pennsylvania Medical School report that as many as two in five achievers feel that they are frauds, inferior in ability and undeserving of success. Despite their considerable accomplishments, they constantly fear being "found out."

BELIEVING IN LOVE

Of course we can, and should, listen to the conversation between Ben and Paul to replace self-defeating and fear-motivated thoughts. More important however, and more basic, is to change who and what we believe in.

BELIEVE IN LOVE, NOT ITS OPPOSITE

God's only Child is Love. We either believe in Him or we believe in His opposite. What we believe in becomes the source of what we expect. What we have faith in produces our expectations. In fact, expectation is faith. Fear is faith in evil. Love is the expression of faith in good (or God).

Both Paul and Ben are empowered by (and dependent upon) either love or fear. If Paul and Ben are empowered by fear, then Paul Ben Solomon lives in hell. It is natural that their faith will be reflected in the content of their conversation (self-talk). When I am willing to place my faith in Love (life, good, God), Paul and Ben as I have known them will die and be reborn. I will expect, believe in and empower love, life, light and good in myself, others and the world around me.

To expect, believe in and empower Love (light, life, Good) in Self and the world is to transform self and the world. All things become possible. All things are made new. Miracles are no longer beyond belief or the power to produce.

CAUSE AND EFFECT PRODUCE REALITY

This is not meant to suggest or encourage attempts to abridge natural law or reality. It awakens the ability to recognize reality without interpretation, judgment or coloration that give power to frustrate or work against me. Even the word "good" here is not used in a context of "good-bad, right-wrong" judgments. It refers to the reality that absolutely everything that happens can and will serve the interests of my life and experience.

Miracles should not be thought of as a magical way to avoid the consequence of natural law. No amount of wishing for a way out or wishing things were different will produce a miracle. Do not wish for more creative power to perform feats of magic and make things better. One who wishes things were different and finds reality unacceptable, is already applying enough creativity to give reality a power that is not inherent. One who describes incidents as "terrible, awful, unacceptable" is giving those incidents power to create misery and suffering.

NO "POLLYANNA" HERE

The suggested alternative is not a "pollyanna" attitude that tries to sweetly accept everything as wonderful and does nothing to create change. The Possible Human approaches life with a knowledge that, "no matter what happens, I can handle it and there is always an alternative to handling it with misery, hurt and despondency."

The Meta-Human goes one further by knowing, "As I am in harmony with God and because natural law serves God, natural law is at my service and does not represent conflict."

The distinguishing feature between The Possible Human and The Meta-Human is that The Possible Human calls upon his natural resources and the ability to think supportively, which provides strength to manage any challenge or obstacle of life but does not necessarily provide the power to transform the challenge or obstacle itself. The Possible Human may even have available tools of prayer and meditation to ask divine assistance. The Possible Human, in fact, may have developed great spiritual power by effectively using the techniques we call prayer and meditation with positive result so that his level of expectancy in using those tools will often produce what The Average Human calls miracles.

The Meta-Human, on the other hand, has developed such a personal relationship with the Source of mind and law that prayer is constant and is so in harmony with the purpose of natural law that "coincidences" and miracles are a regular feature of life.

THE TWO STEPS IN THE TRANSFORMATION PROCESS TO BECOMING A META-HUMAN

WHOLE TRUST

The first step will require your whole trust in Love (Living Love, the expression of God). To assist in taking this step you may want to review the consequence of believing in fear and limitation. You may not appreciate the title "Christ." Don't make that an issue. If you are Jewish, put your trust in the fact that "Israel" means "Prince of God." There can be no Prince unless God has a child. The "Child of God" is obviously the prince and that is "who you really are." The Christians may have an advantage through believing that in a particular time and place, the Messiah demonstrated the power to overcome fear and death. The Messiah has also acted repeatedly through Jewish history, manifesting His power as Living Love enabling extraordinary occurrences to manifest through those who believe in Him and allow Him to manifest.

Start a conversation with Living Love, the Child of God. Allow yourself to sense a presence of a living being, capable of being a close friend and confidant, a teacher, an elder brother or sister. The qualities you recognize in this one are absolute. These qualities include the three aspects of love:

> Kindness/Caring
> Acceptance/Understanding
> Challenge/Service

Qualities not included in this Living Loving Presence:

> Judgment and Condemnation
> Lack and Limitation
> Accusation and Blame
> Punishment

You must become familiar with the voices used by "Paul and Ben," the two sides of yourself. They are not Paul's and Ben's voices, they are the voices of Love and fear.

Fear **never** tells the truth. Any statement that tells you how hopeless things are is not the truth. No statement of your worthlessness is the truth.

RENEWAL

Once you have stated your commitment to faith in Love, renew that faith and commitment regularly.

Listen to the conversation between Paul and Ben (use your own two names). When the content does not come from love, speak to Love immediately: "Love, I want to get to know you better. I ask you to become more real and alive in my life."

As for Paul and Ben, always remember to state your appreciation for each of them whenever they "pop up." When you are aware that Ben would like to do something or have something, but Paul has produced fear and a warning, then speak to Ben first, "I'm glad you're still there as part of my life, Ben." I'm glad I still have the passion and drive to want things and to want to do things. I love you."

Then speak to Paul, "Paul, there you are again, trying to protect my integrity and to remind me of responsibility. I'm so lucky to have you. I'm fortunate that you are so conscientious."

Then, again, speak to love, "Love please teach Ben and Paul a love for one another and a love for you. Please help us to always think and act through love."

FORTY DAYS

I suggest that you deliberately and conscientiously conduct such a conversation (aloud, if possible) every day for at least forty days. And converse with these three beings: your adventurous child, your governor/parent and Love (Christ) as often as you can remember it, every day for the forty days. If you should miss a day, start over without feeling guilty. Just start again until you have consistently nurtured the relationship for forty days.

Do not beg, plead or cry. Do simply accept God as your God. If there are no lights or bells or visions, don't be concerned. This is yours to do. Do it. Claim Love for your own by making a decision. Do it with a certain "knowing," not merely hope. "You are my God, my Christ, even if I don't yet know you well." Then begin your conversation.

I am suggesting that you make this a "one-way" conversation for the Forty Days. During this Forty-Day Experience, do not ask for an answer from Love. Do not ask God to speak. Do not ask for answers. Simply speak to Love.

The purpose of the Forty Days is to allow you to get to know Love as a real Being and as a friend. It is to develop familiarity with this Friend you will often call upon and ask for guidance and assistance. Before you call for guidance and assistance, you must establish as an absolute certainty that the friend you are coming to know has only the qualities of love and support and is not condemning, judgmental or punishing (born of some preacher's wrath). You also need to be certain that your self-talk between Paul and Ben is no longer born of fear and hell. If these two have begun to "automatically" love, accept, appreciate and support one another, you are ready now to allow Love to speak on the forty-first day.

EXERCISE #2: RENDING THE VEIL

You have already noticed that there is a "you" who deeply desires to make a contribution to the world. There is a "you" who wants to love and be loved. There is a "you" who wants it to have mattered that you were alive. "You" want to make a gift to the world.

Almost anyone who will give it a second thought will realize that "You" exists. But you may have "You" well hidden. You are hidden behind a veil of fear. The hidden You is "the You that you would like to be but are afraid you are not." The veil itself is "the you that you believe you are and the you that you are afraid you are." The veil is carefully maintained by attempts to justify your actions and to be right.

Try this sometime soon. Just when you realize you are being argumentative or unkind, jealous or manipulative, stop suddenly. Stop and describe in direct and real terms, without justification, explanation or excuse, that you have just seen what you are doing and that you do not want to do that.

The people you are interacting with will almost certainly be shocked, for two reasons: first, because the action is so unusual, but more importantly, they will suddenly see the You that you really are with the veil stripped away.

What they will see is a strong, honest, loving person who is not willing to participate in unkindness and activity that is not supportive. They will have seen the Christ standing before them. Because you were willing to reveal the smallness of which you are capable, the greatness that You are is revealed.

If you are willing to so reveal to yourself and others the Greatness that You are, you will quickly overcome your lack of self-love, self-worth and alrightness. If rending the veil becomes habit when you recognize acts and attitudes born of fear, you will soon develop confidence, security and strength and will have fewer occasions when the veil needs to be rent in order to reveal the You that You really are.

EXERCISE #3: A MEDITATION ON LOVE AND FORGIVENESS

Allow yourself a reverie in a pleasant place, walking in the sand on a beach with all the ocean sounds and smells and the feel of sand crunching under your feet. Create such a scene in your creative mind and involve yourself as completely as you can.

You will see many people approaching from a distance. In your visualization, allow each to become recognizable.

First, there is a little child. The child looks like you but is laden with heavy rocks. Each great stone weighs the child down under a burden. Each rock represents the weight of a self-condemning belief or accusation or a guilt that your child must carry through life until you lift it. Allow yourself to call to mind the "heavy trips" that you have put upon the child, including those you bought from others. The better you can notice the nature of each, the more effective you will be in lifting them.

Do not be afraid to apologize and reassure the child. "I love you just as you are. You are my beautiful, adventurous child and I want to free you from your burden. I would like us to have fun and enjoy life. I want you to know I love you."

Ask the child to forgive the critical parent and visualize hugging one another. Make a pact to be supportive of one another even when no one else is. Tell your child to always be there for you, even if no one else approves of you, "When others criticize or reject you, I will consider that my special opportunity to tell you that you are alright. I will give to you kindness and caring, acceptance and understanding; I will serve you and your needs and interests, and I will challenge and encourage you to become stronger and more effective even while I remember to accept you just as you are now."

Now bring an image of each of your parents into the picture. Give forgiveness, love, kindness/caring, understanding/acceptance and challenge/service. Allow yourself to feel loved by each of them, even if you never did before. If either has done some unkindness in the past, they were responsible for the act at the time, but you are responsible for keeping it alive now. Forgive and release for your own sake, and even "put words into their mouths," words of apology they do not have the strength to say, words of forgiveness and encouragement. Give them love even if you receive none in return. Prosperously give of your love, because you are so wealthy you can afford to give your love away to those who have not earned it. Say thank you when that is appropriate.

Bring in an authority figure. Visualize someone who has been very difficult to approach. Remember that this person once wore diapers. Visualize this individual in diapers. Talk kindly to the authority figure from your own wealth of love. Be generous to the little child tyrant and give the three aspects of love.

Bring up the image of anyone who needs forgiveness. You can afford to be generous. You have love to give and you are loved whether they love you or not.

CHAPTER XI

The Only Love There Is

"When you have accomplished the ability to love yourself unconditionally, you will automatically be inclined to give unconditional love to others."

THE ONLY LOVE IS UNCONDITIONAL LOVE

Learning to love is a beautiful experience. When I learn to love unconditionally, the world is populated by people I love. When my world is filled with people I love, I feel loved in return and indeed, I will be loved. When I make of love a contest saying in essence, "I will love you if you will love me and meet my requirements," we tend to get into the child's game of "You first," "No, you first." We find ourselves constantly proving our love and requiring others to prove that they love us.

I LOVE YOU BECAUSE

There is no other love than unconditional love. Love that is a return for expectations met is selfish manipulation, not love. The ability to love unconditionally comes from personal security. When I am so confident of my alrightness and when I am sure that I am loved, I can give love freely without even requiring love in return.

It is the experience of saying, "I love you," (and meaning it). "I love you because I want to, not because you've earned it. I love you because it is natural and good. It is a beautiful experience for me and there is no good reason why I should not. I love you and even if you cannot love me it is all right; I am loved. I have taken care of that. I will not feel hostile or hurt if you do not love me. I will simply realize that you have not yet recognized what I am. I am lovable. I know that because I love me and I find that a joyous experience. You are fortunate to receive my love because it is valuable, supportive and worthwhile. I would be fortunate to receive your love because it is a supportive energy that makes our experience together more beautiful. I do want your love. I do care whether you love me, but I will not choose to withhold my love if you do not. I will love you anyway because I want the experience of loving you."

Those who love unconditionally make an automatic assumption upon meeting someone that they will love that person. There is a belief that it is natural and normal to do so and there is little or no reason not to. After all, that person is by nature an intricate, delicate, complex responsive, wonderful creation. I already know that upon meeting. Each of us has some wonderful traits and probably some awful ones. Who has only wonderful traits? I may meet anyone at their worst or at their best. In any case, I know that the best way to relate is to have faith in the good in everyone. I am much more likely to experience the good in our relationship because of that faith.

LOVE IS A HABIT

Most of us have developed a long-standing habit of loving those who love us and who please or entertain us. We have a habit of denying love to those who displease or disappoint us, unless society has dictated special status for them as is true of immediate family. I love someone because it is expected of me.

The habit is strongly reinforced. When we were children before love became habit, we may have responded with "I hate you" when mother or some family member disappointed us. We were told, of course, "That's not nice," and we learned that we are obligated to love certain people. Now that the habit is long-standing, the response seems automatic. We do not likely think it through and make a conscious decision to decide to love him but not her. The response seems automatic and not about love. That is to say, I love not because I decide to, but just because it happens to me. The illusion is created by allowing decisions to be made by habit.

We are creatures of habit. Almost all the feelings and emotions we consider "automatic" are really habits. When I react with anger so suddenly that I do not have time to think, it is because I have a habit.

The element of choice does not seem to exist and I am a victim of my emotions unless I learn to build new habits.

So it is with love. If my love habit dictates that I will distrust those I meet or that love is only for a few special people, I will act "automatically" according to that habit, and I will love few people. If my love habit dictates that I am a loving person and that I automatically extend love to those who will receive it and even secretly to those who will not, I will habitually love. People will find me to be loving.

Habits are replaced by habits. New habits are built by practice. Establishing a new love habit is a matter of making a decision to love, then practicing. It will necessitate reminding myself again and again. I will never meet a person without need for my love. I am a source of love and love is a survival necessity. I have something available that every person in the whole world needs in order to survive. It will not cost me to give it. I will not have less of it when I do. In fact I will have more. The giving of it, the use of it, causes it to multiply.

HOW TO FALL IN LOVE — A SPECIAL WEEKEND

Here is a technique that can be vitally important to use in close relationships. It is especially helpful when there are difficulties in a marriage or close working partnership.

Set aside a weekend to get away from all ordinary activities and challenges of work and family. This is for just the two of you.

Use one of the two days of the weekend for each of you. On your partner's day, let him (or her) do all the talking. Ask questions. Get him to tell his life story in detail. Especially find out all the fears and insecurities he ever felt. What his dreams were. What he felt or wondered about God. How he dealt with challenges. This is his time. Ask him to tell you the things he has felt in his relationship with you but was afraid to say. Be prepared to listen and ask to understand further but DO NOT offer any excuses, explanations or "That's not the way it was." The purpose of this sharing is to learn clearly what he has felt, what his values are, what he would like to do and be. You are plumbing the depths to find ideals, goals, secret ambitions and dreams. Do not talk about your relationship. Talk about him. Listen.

If you are successful in bringing out all that his heart wants to pour out, you will bring out the little child in him and you will open his heart.

The second day, of course, is yours (or you can go first). Don't hold back, especially about your childhood and your dreams, times when you were hurt or afraid, what your fantasies and dreams were, how you have felt and how you feel, what you have wanted and what you want.

Don't discount the magic. If the technique seems too simple, do understand that true communication does not occur in words, it happens in spite of words and is accomplished by the heart. It is virtually impossible to allow someone to pour out their heart to you without allowing yourself to love them.

This technique provides a basis for understanding. It is possible to forgive, understand and accept almost anything in another when you see why it is there.

ONE LAST COMMENT ON LOVE

The magic of unconditional love is that when you have accomplished the ability to love yourself unconditionally, you will automatically be inclined to give unconditional love to others. As you learn to accept, understand and forgive yourself, you will accept, understand and forgive others easily and automatically. When you learn to give yourself kindness and caring, you will be kind to others automatically. When you encourage yourself to meet the challenge of your highest potential, you can support others expressing their greatness. As you learn to let all life serve you and are willing to serve yourself in your own needs by meeting personal responsibility, you will find service easy and rewarding.

CHAPTER XII

Mega-Tools Of The Meta-Human

"One thing that does not necessarily typify the genius is a high I.Q. It is creativity, rather than intelligence, that makes the genius."

There are two primary factors which empower the Meta-Human. The first is the acceptance of Love as the Source of mind and power. It may be a one-time act of noticing that only Love and fear empower thought and making a total commitment to the Love-source. It is at once a commitment and a request. The commitment is to listen to, and draw upon this Source for thought and energy. The request is for this Source to actively provide thought, guidance and the vitality of life.

The second factor is consistent, on-going, conscious and unconscious participation in expressing this Source. The unconscious participation results from the "completeness" of the commitment. When I have so totally placed my belief and faith in Love as my Source of life and thought that I do not have to stop and think whether to draw on it or not, my thoughts, actions and even my dreams are an expression of Love in action. Conscious participation with Living Love has long been called prayer (speaking) and meditation (listening, accepting and receiving).

THE GENIUS MIND

Research into the genius mind has shown that the extraordinary thinking of the great inventor, physicist or master artist differs in some specific ways from the "ordinary" rational, logical thinking process. These qualities of the genius mind have been noted:

TENACITY

One quality of the genius mind is that it will not settle for a "non-answer." The genius mind clings to its challenge with a tenacity that maintains its question like an undercurrent beneath and behind all other activity. But, unlike the average thinker, this underlying question is not maintained as a stress factor that distracts the mind from other pursuits.

MULTI-FACETED

The genius maintains interest in several (often unrelated) pursuits. In fact, a mechanism which seems to work for the genius is a "flash of insight" that often comes this way:

> A genius will become immersed in exploration of a particular challenge until the limit of available information and the conscious ability to apply it is reached. Then, the genius will drop the problem to become just as immersed in a totally unrelated challenge. This unrelated challenge is often a difficult piece of music or art or even contemplation of a sunset. Or it may, in fact, be an unrelated scientific project. The common factor is becoming as totally absorbed with "the diversion" as the genius was with the original question. Suddenly the "flash of insight" comes. Often, the seemingly unrelated challenge takes on relevance and demonstrates the sought-after principle. But, just as often, the understanding appears to "just pop into the mind" as if it were being worked out by some other level of mind while the genius was involved in the unrelated pursuit.

TENSION-RELEASE

Noticeable in the genius mind is the "tension/release" factor. The genius conscientiously applies his available logic and effort. These are applied with tenacity and to a "saturation point." Then, effort is totally released with another "saturation" pursuit.

RELAXATION

It has often been postulated that the power of the creative, intuitive mind is released through relaxation and meditation or by "switching over" from the "left brain" active logic to "right brain" receptivity. Or, similarly, it is released through rhythmic, hypnotic, or simply unrelated activity that "disinhibits the cerebral cortex." Certainly these techniques are applicable. Still more applicable may be a process called "brain integration," including the tension release factor.

OTHER QUALITIES OF THE GENIUS MIND

BELIEF

The genius mind believes in a source of answers and understanding.

This may not be a religious belief, but there is a tenacious belief that an answer will come — not necessarily through the logical process.

DARES TO BE DIFFERENT

The genius thinker is almost always a "renegade." There is a departure from conventional thought and practice. There needs to be self-confidence and a belief in what is being done that allows the genius mind to withstand persecution, disbelief, criticism and ostracism from peers. This is a rare quality indeed.

CURIOSITY

The genius mind wants to know everything and how everything works. This is a quality we have attributed to "the adventurous child" side of self and it suggests that the genius mind is one in which this child has not been subdued by the critical parent.

INTELLIGENCE QUOTIENT

One thing that does not necessarily typify the genius mind is a high I.Q. It is creativity, rather then intelligence, that makes the genius. It would appear that the qualities of the genius mind are available to The Average Human who chooses to apply them. The limits are not physiological or genetic but lie in our willingness to reach beyond accepted limits.

CHAPTER XIII

Brain Integration And Brain Transcendence

BRAIN INTEGRATION AND THE FOUR ELEMENTS

There is a lot of talk these days about brain integration. Most of the talk centers around the discovery that the two hemispheres of the brain are specialized. Current research suggests that the left hemisphere of the brain is primarily concerned with logic and with "the lines that define space," while the right side of the brain is more aware of space and is more intuitive than logical. According to researchers, the left brain is more rational, reasonable, adult-like. It is the teacher, the one who figures things out logically and may inhibit the more impulsive right side of the brain.

The right brain seems more child-like, imaginative and creative. It may be that if the left brain didn't exist, the right brain would just believe in everything. It loves fairy tales. It loves legends and symbols, though it may have no idea what symbols really mean, at least not logically; it has a "feeling" for them. When it hears about miracles and heroes, knights in shining armor, angels, and things of heaven, it may have no problem accepting that as reality.

When the right brain gets carried away with fantasies about reincarnation, past lives, space ships, fairies and wondrous things, the left brain reacts, "Wait a minute. Careful who you say those things to. Don't let people know you believe in that. Don't get caught up in fantasy. Don't let your adventure take over. Don't be too child-like."

DRAWING ON THE RIGHT SIDE OF THE BRAIN

There was a flurry of attention a few years ago when Betty Edwards, an art teacher at UCLA, published a book called **Drawing On The Right Side Of The Brain.** She reported that inhibiting input from the left brain could actually improve drawing skills. Students drew "upside down" and with their drawing pads covered so "the left brain" could not see what their hands were doing. They were taught relaxation exercises and the right-brain drawings displayed uninhibited talent. Soon there was a rash of books on activities ranging from tennis and golf to investing, drawing from the right side of the brain.

Carol Austin, an art teacher at the University of Humanistic Studies in San Diego, California, independently discovered that "brain integration" improved her art skill and that of her students. Carol's work did not focus on shifting control from the left brain to the right brain, but rather focused on balancing what she describes as the four major components of the brain.

THE LEFT BRAIN

People who are left-brain dominant are also called "earth" types, referring to that solid, down-to-earth, reasonable, logical quality. In the extreme they are "computerish," giving emphasis to the facts while excluding consideration for feelings or persons.

It is the adult side, the part that makes things "solid" and gives them defined boundaries. This earth part may be what gives person integrity, a foundation on which to stand.

THE RIGHT BRAIN

Right-brain dominant people are called "water" types. They are more yielding, serving, understanding, and perhaps also "wishy-washy" and placating. Their decisions are more likely to be based on intuitive feelings, and they may not be able to explain any reason for doing what they are doing.

THE PRIMITIVE BRAIN

At the base of the brain is the primitive brain, the reptilian brain, the brain stem. This part of the brain is instinctive and is the seat of the primal mind. It may have characteristics of a wild animal living in the wilderness, and has developed instinctual responses. Animals survive by learning what to fear. Wild animals are "skittish." When they feel trapped or hurt, they are likely to lash out viciously at anyone who goes near.

The primitive part of the mind is much like the wild animal. It is characterized by the element of fire. It is passionate, involved in life, yet is fearful and skittish. It is not rational or logical, and reacts rather than tries to figure things out.

People who are "primal dominant" tend to be incendiary at the slightest provocation. They release their fire like an explosion because they are motivated by fear. Instinct rules their lives and often they can hardly be accused of thinking at all. They just sort of react.

WE ARE ALL THREE AND MORE

You probably recognize all three in yourself. You may be thinking, "Am I left brain, right brain or am I primal?" You are likely to be dominant in one or another type of thinking, but you are all three and more. Sometimes you are left brain dominant, and sometimes, especially if you are not winning an argument using your right-brain imagination, you'll speak from your left brain and say, "Never mind how I feel. Never mind how you feel. Just the facts, I want this: one, two, three, four. Just a list of the facts, please." Of course, if the other person does that better than you, then you run back to the right brain and confuse the issue with feelings. We use all these parts of the brain.

WANDERING THROUGH THE WILDERNESS

We enter life through the primitive gateway, the place of the instinct, the animal world where the primal brain dominates. We are then thrust into a computer-like process in which imagination and logic, the right and left brain, compete, both claiming to be the "true voice" of self. The result is often a wilderness of confusion.

As input comes from the five senses into these three brain parts, we begin to attempt to sort out the confusion by making decisions and establishing values. We set goals in life, and determine how we will attain them.

We observe, make comparisons, and draw conclusions with the left brain. But often the right brain disagrees with those conclusions. We have a "feeling" that is not "logical," in fact, it may disagree with logic. Conflict results, the primal brain gives its input and fear enters the decision-making process. The result is confusion. There is something we want to do, but we are afraid.

Added to the confusion are beliefs formed by other people's opinions. These beliefs are often based on frightening or painful situations we experienced early in life. We took the values of adult care-takers and made them beliefs.

All this is the wilderness, and some of us spend lifetimes wandering through it.

UNITING FIRE AND AIR WITH EARTH AND WATER

The element of air is the fourth part of the active brain. It results from "disinhibiting the cerebral cortex." We may disinhibit the cerebral cortex (where most of our thinking takes place),by doing things that make us "light, carefree and joyful." Often chanting, singing, dancing or moving rhythmically will disinhibit the cerebral cortex.

A person who is an "air type" is light and free. In the most positive expression, they are joyous and relieve heavy moments with laughter. They also can be irrelevant, cool, and unresponsive.

The place of air ("inside" or under the cerebral cortex) is separated from the place of fire (the brain stem) by the places of earth and water (the left and right hemispheres).

When the fire of your vitality is held back by earth, it is suppressed with reasons, justifications, rules, and limitations. You can become like a smoldering volcano.

When this fire is inhibited by your watery, emotional self, it disperses into fantasies and emotional reactions and it releases, rarely grounding itself to practical applications that can "give it fuel" and direction. The water puts out the fire, and you wonder why your dreams never become reality.

BRAIN INTEGRATION

When your earth and water — right and left brain, your grandiose child and your parent self — no longer battle for control, but are supportive of one another, your passion can rise, with the integrity of earth and the creativity of water, to an expanded perception of who you really are. This fire of passion will blend with the air element of understanding and come to life, uniting all four elements in harmony and a spectacular release of joy. Those who teach brain integration focus on harmonizing the right and left brain hemispheres into balance. There are several techniques for accomplishing this including some forms of meditation, the techniques of Super-Learning[1] that use largo rhythms of baroque music during the learning process and such machines as The Graham Potentializer. There are also body"alignment" techniques such as Alpha Biotics and devices that impart sound with a hertz differential (110 hertz sound impulses played into one ear, 100 hertz sound impulses played into the other ear through a headphone with a differential of 10 hertz is said to be an ideal ratio). These include the Hemi-Sync TM techniques of Robert Monroe[2] and instruments such as Inner Quest that use light and sound to produce hemispheric synchrony.

Results obtained by these techniques are truly amazing. It is said to improve concentration, accelerate learning and heighten creativity, as well as enhance self-healing.

All this is within reach of The Possible Human.

BRAIN TRANSCENDENCE — THE RELEASE OF FIRE

Average Humans contain their fire for a whole lifetime, intending someday to invest that fire in something. Then they die, which means that the fire went out. They worked for fifty years to make a living, but didn't get around to making a life. The people who do release their fire into a particular pursuit are those people who make history. The person who has released his fire has answered the question of the purpose of life, has freed himself from the wilderness of confusion, and has come forth into the Promised Land.

That person will have an effect on you, no matter what the area of his talent or direction. A musician who is full of fire will affect you with his music. An artist full of fire will affect you with his art. A writer full of fire will affect you with what he writes, no matter what the subject. Wherever you've released your fire is an outlet for power. The few people who have totally released their fire have been transformed beings.

THE FIRE OF THE ANCIENTS

The Mystery Schools of ancient India spoke of the kundalini fire. The Mystery Schools of the Far East spoke of the chi as fire. The Hebrew school of the prophets spoke of the Shekhina fire. The Egyptian Mystery Schools described the left and right hemispheres, the brain stem and the mind beyond the brain (the Holy place that could not be contained within the earthly temple). These Mystery Schools spoke of The Crown of Divine Fire. Allow me to draw from these ancient Mystery Schools with the following description of releasing the Divine Fire:

Tantra Yoga describes a chakra[3] system within and around the human body. The chakras are described as vortices of energy that provide life force to animate the body/brain/mind. The chakras have a counterpart in all the other Mysteries. The Christian Mysteries speak of "seals" in John's Revelation. The Tantric and Greek Mysteries describe the "cadeusius" within (and around) the body. The seven levels, wheels, seals or chakras are also found in the Kabala of Hebrew Mysticism.

THE CADEUSIUS UPON THE "HUMAN BODY," THE TEMPLE IN MAN

The two serpents in the drawing are called the Ida and the Pingala. The rod in the center is called the Shushumna. These are also the Pillar of Mercy (right hand pillar or serpent), the Pillar of Severity, (left hand Pillar) and the Middle Pillar.

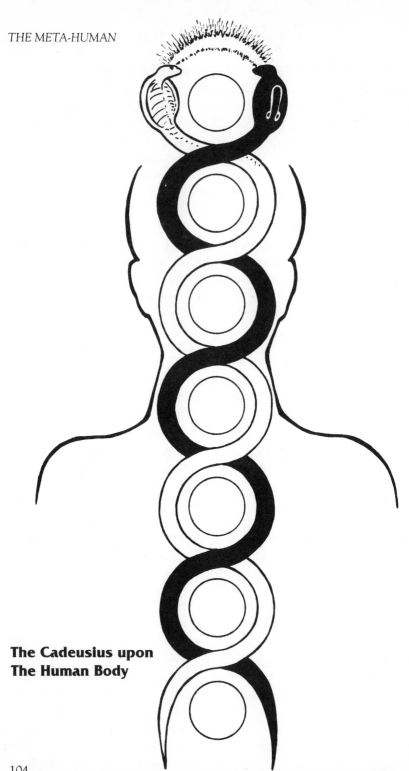

**The Cadeusius upon
The Human Body**

The Mysteries speak of these as a positively charged serpent (right side), a negatively charged serpent (left side), and a rod of crystal (center). It is worth noting that a ruby rod, wrapped with electrically charged wires that cross at seven points is a diagram for a laser. The laser light projects a beam from the ruby rod. The Tantric Yoga declares that when energy is brought through the middle pillar (rod or Shushumna), the "electrical charge" travels through the serpents and when it reaches the head of each serpent, there is an arc of light and "electricity" that flashes from the head of one to the other. This produces a "pool of light," or a "crown of light," rather than a beam as produced by the laser, but of the same relative intensity. This "Crown of Divine Light" is Enlightenment.

YOUR CROWN OF DIVINE LIGHT

The Mysteries declare that "if the eye is single, the whole body is filled with light."[4] This Mystery refers to the above condition in which the fire is released in an integrated brain, but with one additional step. This additional step is what creates The Meta-Human from The Possible Human. That step is "accessing the Divine Mind" in addition to total (four part) brain integration. The eye being single is what John called, "make straight your path." He means that singleness of purpose (to be one with God) invokes the Divine Mind that is "extra-brain." It is one step beyond brain integration. This is accessing the Divine Mind, the ultimate "Mega-tool" of the Meta-Human.

CHAPTER XIV

A Guided Experience In Spiritual Evolution

"When your fantasy involves two or more of the subtler senses simultaneously, you have effectively entered a separate reality."

INNER LIGHT CONSCIOUSNESS

For the past several years I have enjoyed presenting a thirty-hour guided experience in spiritual evolution called Inner Light Consciousness. The experience brings together a number of practical concepts, techniques and exercises for brain integration and effective living. The centerpiece is an effective exercise in applying the super tools for communication and communion with the Source of life and mind.

In this chapter we offer this focal method of Inner Light Consciousness as an effective tool for tapping the Meta-mind. For best results, you invoke the qualities of the genius mind in all that you do, following this guideline:

1. CURIOSITY — Deliberately arouse your curiosity concerning all things. Want to know. Encourage your desire to know and understand. Be curious about how things work and what they are. Free your curiosity to understand what makes a computer work and how plants grow. Read interesting research material about the body and the mind and about the world we live in.

2. MULTI-FACETED — Take on two or more important projects that demand study, exploration and cleverness. Pick two or more real challenges. Your interest in these must be genuine, so pick two in which you would like to actually contribute. Make a difference in how these things are understood or done. Give yourself a reason to be a Meta-Human.

3. TENACITY — Make a commitment to results in these projects. Evoke that classical tenacity of a genius at work who would die trying or refuse to die until the answer has come, until the project has yielded.

4. TENSION-RELEASE — Involve your energy in one or more of the projects to a saturation point, and when you feel you cannot deal with it any further, go on at least one step beyond saturation.

5. DARE TO BE DIFFERENT — Conventional approaches and orthodox thinking may not yield results. Listen to what experts are saying is the "only" approach and look instead for an approach that is unorthodox. Look for answers in strange places.

6. A WAY OF LIFE — These challenges you have accepted are not arbitrary. You have challenges that are part of your everyday life which need extraordinary wisdom and understanding. Apply all the genius qualities to everything you do, including your leisure. Challenge your opportunities and your problems to yield extraordinary results.

Having approached life in this manner, you are ready to apply the "mega-tools."

AWAKEN THE SUBTLER SENSES

There are at least five subtler senses or inner senses that are subtler counterparts of our five senses. These subtler senses are commonly used for memory and reverie. When these senses are used to recognize an actual event taking place at a distance, or to convey information not available to the external senses, they are referred to as clairvoyance (subtler sight), clairaudience (subtler hearing) or clairsentience (subtler feeling). The development and use of these subtler senses is neglected by The Average Human for several reasons:

1. We are taught not to believe information received through these senses ("It's just your imagination").

2. We believe that it is impossible.

3. Religions teach that it is "of the devil." (Imagine believing in the devil to give us useful senses.)

4. Fear (upon which all the above reasons are based):

A result of neglecting to use the subtler senses is that many people cannot even recognize the content of their own "self-talk" the thoughts, ideas and beliefs that are the source of disease and self-sabotaging behavior.

It is worthwhile to actually practice using the subtler senses.
For example:

Close your eyes and "see" as clearly as you can the face of a
loved one. Look carefully at every detail. Care deeply for the
one you are visualizing. Care enough to sense how that person
feels.

With your eyes closed, remember the sound of favorite
music. Listen for particular instruments, blending voices.
Remember and listen to the sound of a song bird, the rustling of
leaves, the sound of water in a brook.

Recall and re-create what a flower petal feels like. "Feel" a
leaf, the bark of a tree, your lover's skin, the flesh of a baby after
a bath.

Great creators, inventors and scientists have "seen" a diagram, a
picture of the resolution of a current challenge. The great composer
Schumann "heard" whole melodies already written. These great genius
minds who participated regularly in reveries involving more than one of
the subtler senses had made these senses available as communication
devices to receive instruction.

A SEPARATE REALITY

There is more of reality than can be experienced by the five external senses. It is suggested by some, in fact, that all exists first in a
creative (separate) reality. The process of creative writing, composing or
inventing could be described as using the mind to transpose from
creative to material reality.

AN EXERCISE IN CREATING A SEPARATE REALITY

After you have exercised the subtler senses, you may want to experiment with experiencing a subtler reality. When a fantasy involves more
than one of the subtler senses simultaneously, you have effectively
entered a separate reality. The reality you experience in a given moment
is that which predominantly occupies your mind. If you can successfully
forget the room in which you are sitting and give all your attention to
what you are "seeing" and "hearing," "feeling" and "smelling" in another
setting, the reality you experience in that moment is the one your senses
are focused upon.

This can serve several purposes:

The transference of your consciousness to a separate reality allows an "opposite saturation" focus from concentration; by totally removing your thought and awareness from your body, it allows a perfect physical and mental relaxation process to occur.

By creating one particular separate reality that you visit often, the specific images and colors, sounds and senses of that particular reality become a "trigger mechanism" for the specific purpose assigned to it.

For example:

If you create a beautiful meadow with lush green grass, a brook flowing through and mountains in a distance, clouds overhead, the sound of birds and of water, the smell of fresh country air and of wild flowers, then you consecrate this place as a special inner sanctum for spiritual attunement. Because the specific place with a specific appearance is associated with your spiritual, inspirational sense, that sense will be evoked each time you return.

I do recommend that you set aside another forty days for this experience. During this forty-day period, each day stretch and breathe for a few minutes. Fill your lungs from bottom to top and release in a sigh of relaxation. Then, using one subtler sense at a time, begin to see your special meadow. Visualize it in detail. Not just fields of grass, but an individual blade of grass casting its shadow on another. Notice tints and hues of color; look at textures and shapes. Notice the landscape layout where paths are and where the brook is.

Having saturated the first sense (visualization), now add another sense. Not functioning separately, the second sense needs to be experienced simultaneously with the first. Add your sense of smell. Smell the wild flowers. When you are experiencing two subtler senses at the same time, you add dimension to your reality. You will also, of course, occupy more of your mind and relax further, drawing your attention away from distraction in the sensory reality.

Now add a third sense. Listen for the sound of the bubbling, gurgling, singing brook as water trickles over rocks and into a small waterfall.

Practice being able to experience all five senses at once. See the brilliant colors of a butterfly. Taste a wild strawberry. Smell the freshness of the air after a spring shower. Touch the bark of a tree. Listen to a bird singing.

Now make a dedication in your own words, such as "This is my private Inner Sanctum. No one else can ever know what my Inner Sanctum is like unless invited here by me. This is a place where I come to know Living Love (God) better and to know myself better. I come here to be quiet and safe in all conditions of life. Here is my 'inner study' where I come for insight, guidance, direction and inspiration. This meadow will have any quality I give it. I will not come here casually. I will speak first to Love and say, "I am coming to be with you in the innermost place where you live within me."

Now make a commitment to visit this holy place every day at the same time of day, if possible. This conditioning will serve you very well in creating spiritual discipline. Apart from this sacred meditation time every day, "I will come here only when I have troubles or challenges or when I need to give or receive healing. I will always have a specific purpose and will not use my meadow carelessly."

Practice using your Subtler Senses and your Personal Meadow every day for forty days. Evoke all five subtler senses at the same time so that the mind is totally occupied with this single reality.

When you have completed your forty-day period to establish the Separate Reality and awaken the Subtler Senses, you may then be ready to visit the Sacred Mountain.

Please note: If either of the above did not work for you, or if you skipped even one day of the forty days, please start over! This is a serious request. The effectiveness of these exercises will require a full forty days of practice and preparedness before proceeding.

THE SACRED MOUNTAIN

Every ancient cosmology had its sacred mountain. These mountains were nearly always described as having seven levels with a great cloud and a temple or palace at the top. The Mountain is Shambala; it is Sinai, Valhalla, Olympus, the New Jerusalem. It is Asgard; it is the City of the Golden Gates of Atlantis. All are archetypes of this sacred mountain.

Researchers have identified seven "kinds" of intelligence. Metaphysics teaches seven levels of consciousness. The "Secret of the Golden Flower," a Taoist text, puts seven golden steps leading to the mountain palace of the divine emperor who sits upon a throne in "the square inch [third eye] within the square foot [the face]."

I suggest you set aside twenty minutes a day, every day during the forty-day period, to create this "Jacob's Ladder." On the first seven days:

Stretch, breathe, relax. Close your eyes and awaken each of your subtler senses, creating and entering your meadow in the process. Taste the water in the brook, dangle your feet in the water, and feel the cool wetness. Don't just imagine it, make it real! To make it real will require the use of all five senses simultaneously.

Remind yourself, this is a sacred place. I come here because I am serious about growth and I want to know God and Love.

Now notice before you a spectacular sacred mountain. It stretches up to the sky in seven levels, each a great terrace with a lush garden, each garden a different color. We will follow the color spectrum from red at the base terrace, to orange, yellow, green, blue, purple and white at the top.

The top of the mountain is obscured by a cloud but light is streaming from behind the cloud.

Allow yourself to experience this mountain with all your subtler senses and a sense of awe, if you can manage it. This is a staircase to heaven.

Having seen the spectacularly colorful mountain, prepare yourself to ascend it. Ask permission first. Speak to the highest and best within you. Speak with Love. Ask for assistance in climbing this great mountain.

Walk across the meadow one step at a time. Do this deliberately. Do not watch yourself doing it. Get into the subtler body (look down to see your hands), then walk a step at a time to approach the first great red garden. Rose bushes are showing off deep red roses amidst the shiny green of their leaves. Smell a rose, touch a leaf, feel the texture. Feel a thorn. Notice a sword buried in stone.

The sword buried in stone is your key to climbing to the mountain top. It can only be released by one who, in this moment, has made a decision to exchange old lovers for new. That is to say, "I am making a choice between my spiritual quest and all other wants and ambitions." The sword is released to the worthy.

If you can release the sword, you will free a sense of expectancy that says, "I really expect to be changed by this experience." Allow this same test to occur every day when you come here. It is even wise to pray, "Do not allow me to receive the sword from the stone until I am ready." Do not complete the trek up the mountain unless you can release the sword.

The sense of excitement and expectancy is the power and potency that will empower you to reach the top, in truth and to claim further weapons (tools) there.

You have the sword. Proceed climbing over rocks, brambles and ledges you must make your way past. Keep active and involved. You will climb to a garden that is predominantly orange. Perhaps marigolds bloom here. This is a place to strip away old habits and old self-images. Consider for a moment what you have been saying to yourself and about yourself. "I'll discard the old clothes of thought here, giving myself forgiveness, and release the past." Put on new robes of light and proceed to the yellow sunlit garden in new radiant clothing of light. Feel yourself shine like a light with new strength, power and purity, having left guilt behind.

On the fourth level you will meet your Source, your Christ walking through the ancient trees. In this green garden a cool light is filtering through the trees, and there is a carpet of pine needles and moss on the ground. Ferns grow among the old trees. You may only sense the presence, you need not see Him. Ask here to know Living Love as a friend, teacher and protector. Ask to know the child God gave birth to. Should you find a child being born within you, take the child up to the top of the mountain with you. Should you find a wise, adult being with the feel of an older brother or sister, Master, or teacher, follow behind him. If you only feel the presence of the Love, embrace it and ask for guidance. If you feel no presence at all, accept Love as yours (even without evidence) and cause yourself to feel accepted as you release your old self to become new.

Now travel together as you ask Love to lead you to the top of the mountain. On the blue garden you will find an altar, with blue bells and corn flowers and lapis stones in the path. On the altar, place all things or ideas that might prevent your wholly knowing the Will of Your Source. Leave here your preferences, fantasies and ambitions. You will really sacrifice nothing. Whatever is the will of Love for you is more, not less than you could have wished for. It is here you ask for greater strength and sight.

Now you face the purple garden of responsibility and gratitude. If you will accept responsibility for what you are inspired to do and will do it with all your might, the clouds will part so that you may proceed to the mountaintop for a clearer view of the world and your life.

If you have taken twenty minutes a day to experience fully each of the seven gardens, you will reach the top in one week.

Now build a temple on the mountain-top. Build it amid breathtaking fields of white flowers. The temple is a symbol of the temple in you in which God lives. Love will lead you into the place. Make it spectacular! Spare no expense! Create a great, beautiful, important temple to house the God within.

Ask permission to enter, then sit quietly in the peace that dwells within. Do not ask for an answer to a question, not just yet. Speak to Love and the Source of love, every day for a week. Just say, "Love, I want to get to know you better. I want love to be the power of my life. I believe that love is stronger than fear and I want love to tell me what to do and to teach me to love."

Now listen. Do not listen for words necessarily. Listen for a sense of being filled with energy, of being refreshed. Do not listen for the answer to your question, instead, give "saturation" interest to the accoutrements of the temple. Study your new place to know God. Install a "hot line" telephone to God, if you are so inclined. God seems to like creative people who make ways of effectively communicating. You must remember that God is a good communicator. He made ears and the tongue. He knows how to communicate. Give opportunities. Wait a week before asking questions. Develop a familiarity.

Create a healing room in which you may beam your love and your vitality to give life into the cells of your loved ones. Call on Living Love the Great Physician, to direct your love for healing toward yourself or another, asking at the same time to understand better how to help.

When you descend the mountain, bring peace and love with you. Be willing to spend the rest of your day giving the three aspects of love to those you meet:

Kindness/Caring
Acceptance/Understanding
Challenge/Service

CHAPTER XV

The Planetary Mystery School

I believe that my entire life has been spent carefully planning for the job that I was born to do in this lifetime. I didn't consciously participate in all of the careful guidance and development, however. My conscious participation probably began in 1972, when I discovered the truth of something I had believed as a child.

I am the son of a Southern Baptist minister. I grew up hearing that one could talk with God and get answers. I literally believed that God was part of our family, and that we could talk with Him and He could talk with us. After college, I went to a Southern Baptist Seminary to become a Baptist pastor. I probably would have followed in the family tradition of preachers, but when I finished seminary, my wife left me. I became a member of an extinct species—the divorced Southern Baptist preacher. I was angry with God. I went on a ten-year rebellion trip that was self-destructive. I did all the things a nice Southern Baptist young man would never do.

Eventually I stopped running away and discovered through an amazing series of events that God can literally speak to us, and through us in terms so precise that there is no mistaking the message. It was the beginning of a new dimension in my spiritual experience that had nothing to do with religion as I had known it. In fact it didn't have to do with the god I had known. This was a new God, a greater God. Someone far beyond any concept I'd known before.

I began a period of seeking, discovering, reading and trying to be more informed. The most exciting concept I discovered was in the stories of The Ancient Mystery Schools.

Nothing has ever intrigued me more than the idea that somewhere hidden in a forest or on a mountain where nobody could find it (unless he were enlightened) was a Mystery School.

In this very special school were masters, those who had extraordinary knowledge of the arts and sciences and spiritual cultures and who had perfected their character beyond anyone else on the planet. This was a place where masters taught the secrets of life and death, wisdom and knowledge.

The description said that no one could even make application to such a place. You could only handle your experiences in life so well that one of these masters would discover you, and through his influence, you could be accepted. There your consciousness would be molded through a series of initiations, and you would have the opportunity to grow as fast as a human could grow because of the way in which the lessons were presented.

More than anything else, I wanted to discover one of these schools. Everything in the literature referred to schools of centuries ago, in the time of Pythagoras in Greece or Hermes and Ra in Egypt. Yet there were sometimes hints that The Mystery Schools still exist today.

I did everything I could to get myself ready. But how do you know when you are ready? How can you be sure that the talent scout is going to find you? As impatient as I was, it was not easy to leave these things to blind faith.

With this constantly in the back of my mind, I went about my work with The Fellowship of the Inner Light.

One day a woman I had helped through a crisis was doing volunteer work at The Fellowship. She told me of a Zen Master who taught bonsai, the art of cultivating miniature trees.

"I have a feeling that what he is teaching has little to do with bending and wiring trees," she said. "I do not know what he is really teaching and he will not say. You really should see what he is doing."

I was not really interested in bonsai, but she convinced me to pay a visit. Although I had directions to the school, I drove up and down a narrow country road several times before I found it. There was no street sign. Finally I saw a small building, hidden back in the woods so you would not see it unless you knew it was there.

I knocked on the door. There was no response. I walked behind the building and entered a magical world of miniature trees and forests. Some looked like pines you might see on a cliff beside the ocean, the branches gnarled and windswept by sea breezes and bare white on one side with salt spray. I could see little forests with scores of trees growing from a single stone.

In fact, the forest might include a mountain, a lake and a cliff, a miniature world by itself.

A little old man appeared and invited me to walk through the garden. As we walked, I noticed some peculiar things about him. He was never in a hurry. In fact, he moved so slowly it was as if he were moving through molasses or honey. I was so excited with all that was around me that I would ask three questions before he would answer one. As I moved faster with impatience, he seemed to move even more slowly. The slower he moved the more impatient I became. He didn't seem to notice my frustration. His attention was fixed on the living world around him, communicating with the trees in much the manner you or I would speak to each other. Before we finished our tour, I felt he was apologizing to the garden for my presence.

It was then that I began to realize this man was teaching me something, but not by pointing it out to me. I even had the option of not noticing the lesson. We sat down to chat about his school of bonsai. He spoke as slowly as he moved and leisurely sipped green tea from a tiny cup, and all the while he didn't seem to notice the students going about their work of potting trees. He continued to sip long after I had finished my little cup of tea.

Then, a startling thing happened. I noticed that suddenly he was not there anymore. He had caught the hand of a student who was about to clip a large limb from a tiny tree. He had literally moved so quickly that I did not see him leave his seat before he was touching the girl's hand. "You must warn the tree before you cut," he said, "or it will bleed. Speak to the tree. It must know your intention or it will think you mean harm with those great pruners."

Then, to another student, he said, "Don't you see, if you put a rock there, it will conflict with the direction of the branch. You are creating conflict with this plant. You will not create conflict in the plant if you have no conflict within you. Just be quiet for a moment and resolve your inner conflict." And to another, he said, "Don't think of this as just a plant. Think of it as a soul that needs to be molded in a particular direction. These training wires are like karmic experiences that mold its nature into a more beautiful expression."

As I listened to the bonsai master giving these spiritual truths, it suddenly occurred to me — he is not really teaching horticulture, or botany, or even bonsai. He is teaching spiritual growth and the laws of the universe! What a brilliant mind; so slow and so understated, acting as if he were not brilliant!

As he sat again, I said, " I know you are not going to tell me you are a teacher of spiritual growth, but I can see that you are, and I want to learn from you." He looked at me with a gaze that could melt steel. For a moment I froze, not knowing what to say. But his face softened, and in his very slow, gentle way he said, "I am not a spiritual teacher. I do not

117

believe in spiritual lessons." I thought, "How peculiar. I wonder what he does believe in?" But I didn't quite know how to ask. Hesitantly, I questioned him again, "What do you mean? I know that you are teaching more than how to torture these little trees."

He answered wisely, "If I were a spiritual teacher, I would be teaching spiritual lessons rather than lessons of life. That suggests that I would separate spiritual life from its expression. That produces death. This is not a school of death. It is a school of life. I do not rip things apart. Growth is growth. I do not believe there is any such thing as a spiritual teacher. If a person separates spirit from body he would be teaching an error from the beginning."

Duly impressed, I asked him if he would teach me. "Let's work with a tree for a few moments, and then talk about it," he said. He gave me a rag-tag pine tree that didn't look like bonsai at all. It had thousands of little brown needles, tiny needles because the tree had been miniaturized. He gave me a small pair of tweezers and told me to pick out the brown needles. I am not so dense that I can't recognize a lesson in patience. So I kindly took the tweezers and said, "If it kills me I am going to do it." I picked out little brown needles one by one for hours, wondering all the time if I really had to do it, or whether if he thought it up just for me. As I continued plucking, I kept thinking of all the things I needed to do back at the Fellowship. The more I plucked, the more my thoughts raced, "He should be talking to me. He could be teaching me fantastic lessons while I'm plucking these damn little needles!"

He let it go on for hours, and I did not think he would ever get back to me. When he finally did, I had developed quite a relationship with the tree. I was beginning to see it in a completely different way. Finally, he sat with me and began to comment on my work. He said, "If you were going to shape that into a more beautiful shape, what would you do?"

I looked at some other trees that the bonsai master had shaped, but I did not see how I could work this poor dying specimen into anything resembling one of his masterpieces. "If I bent these branches, or cut them back, it still would not do it. I just don't know." The bonsai teacher did not say anything. He just stared at the tree. I suggested, "Well, maybe it's a windswept, because most of the branches grow in one direction." With his eyes still focused on the tree, he suggested "Why don't we just work on it for awhile and see what happens."

I watched him push the branches around for a few minutes, peering at the tree from every direction. Then he took the pruning shears and began cutting. When he finished the pruning, he wrapped wire around the main trunk and twisted it sharply, forcing the tree to hold a gnarled, windblown appearance. Seeing the general direction of the pruning, I took the shears and started to cut a branch.

I thought he would jump through the ceiling, "Don't cut that yet! You did not ask permission!"

With the jaws of the pruning shears frozen at the base of the branch, I said, "What do you mean?"

He said gently, "The tree is alive. Talk to it. You must explain your intentions before it will cooperate. It's spirit will tell you what direction to go in."

I thought, "Oh, you are going to tell me how to talk to devas!" The idea really excited me, "What do I do?"

His eyes narrowed, "Just talk to it." I looked at that scruffy old pine tree and drew a blank. I did not have any idea how that pine tree was going to talk back to me. There is nothing harder than trying to talk out loud to a tree, and feeling it is just a tree, but I tried. I asked the poor thing what direction it wanted to be trained in. I felt ridiculous. The Bonsai master's face remained blank. Yet behind his disciplined composure, I sensed his amusement at my obvious discomfort.

Finally he said, "If you could see that tree as a human being, what would that being look like?" I began to describe a dirty, skinny little girl with combat boots and uncombed hair. "Close your eyes," he said. "See the little girl standing before you." That was easy enough. I closed my eyes and I could see the little girl.

The bonsai master leaned close to me and whispered, "Now talk to her. Don't talk to the tree. Talk to the little girl. Ask her what she wants."

The thought that came was, "You've already washed my face. Take your instruments and comb my hair." I opened my eyes, and saw the tree from a whole new perspective. It was a different tree altogether, and it was excited as I. The spirit of the tree no longer feared for its life when I cut her branches. It was more like a girl who is getting a haircut, and when the stylist is finished she knows she's going to look beautiful. By the end of the day, what was once an "ugly duckling," was now an exquisitely beautiful windswept pine, with the bark missing on one side. We painted the bare trunk with lime so that it looked as if it had been bleached with salt spray. Looking at it, you could almost smell the ocean. I was thrilled. I felt as if I had seen the transformation of a soul, taking something wild and out of control, and creating living art, beautified by nature itself.

Afterwards I said, "I have always wanted to be a student in a mystery school. I have an idea that you can cause me to learn more in one year than I can learn with my spiritual group in ten. Will you take me as a project, shape my consciousness like yours and mold me as the masters did in the ancient mystery schools?"

He looked at me straight in the eyes and said, "Paul, could you leave your Fellowship, close its doors, and come here as my servant, wash my teacups in my kitchen, make my bed, sweep my floors and pick the needles off scruffy pines? Could you do it, even if I never say anything wise to you, if I never entertain you?" The question hit like a ton of bricks. The Fellowship was my child, a living being, something that was a part of me, and to close it would be like ending a part of my life. But there was another possibility. It seemed to me that the Fellowship would continue even if its doors were closed.

I said, "Yes, I will come and be your servant."

Looking away, he said, "That being true, I cannot teach you." I wasn't expecting that reply, and with tears running down my face I said, "Why?"

He gave two reasons. "For one thing you're too emotional. Secondly, if you could close your Fellowship and come here, then I have need to learn from you. I couldn't close this school and come to stay in your Fellowship."

I learned more in that short exchange than I might have in a lifetime. I had touched the periphery of a mystery school, and it had affected me profoundly. I asked the bonsai master if I could meet his teacher some day. He answered, "If he wants to meet you, he will."

I went home to meditate and to think. I didn't want to miss this opportunity. Finally, I reached for a book, just to quiet my mind. The book opened to a famous story of Annie Besant applying as a student to Madame Blavatsky. She had asked repeatedly, and was turned away. Finally Annie packed her bags, let herself in the great teacher's back door and began to clean and cook a meal for Madame Blavatsky. I closed the book. I knew what I would do.

I called a friend who worked with me at The Fellowship. I said, "I am going away, and I do not know when I will return." I packed a few things and early the next morning let myself in the back door of the teacher's little house in the wood. To my surprise, I found a note in the kitchen giving instructions in how to make tea and prepare breakfast.

A few years later, we moved The Fellowship of The Inner Light to Virginia Beach. One day I received a phone call from a man at the Norfolk Botanical Gardens who said he knew the bonsai master from whom I had learned. He asked if he could show me a tree he had been working with so that I could make some suggestions.

He brought a beautiful little tree that was still in training wires. He sat and we looked at it for a bit. I noticed that the man was oriental. We talked for a few minutes about bonsai techniques, and he departed, leaving the tree in my care.

I thought the tree was a gift from my bonsai teacher in Atlanta, so I called to thank him. When I spoke to him, he said, "I did not give that tree to you." So I asked who did.

"He did."

"Why should one of your students want to give me a tree?"

He replied, "That was not my student, that was my teacher."

My God, I had spent ten minutes with a master and had not asked him a single question! I had waited years to meet this teacher, and I did not have sense enough to recognize him!

I immediately phoned Norfolk Botanical Gardens. I told the teacher I was not quite sure how to care for the plant, and asked if I could see him again. I did not tell him that I had discovered he was a teacher. Very graciously he consented to come again.

Sitting with the tree, he said, "As I was training this branch, instead of easily bending in a new and beautiful direction, it was stiff and ready to break. That was during the period when you decided to teach, instead of publishing your work." I stammered, "How did you know about those incidents in my life?"

He quietly replied, "This tree was put in training wires at the time my student told me about you, and since then I have watched you in the branches of this tree. Everything that you did was reflected in this image of you. If I had resistance from a branch I knew that you were having resistance in what you were doing in your life."

I realized that every branch of the tree had been a point of communication between the teacher and me, and that he had been teaching me for three years. I had never met him, yet he was participating in every incident of my life. He never forced me to learn anything. He never manipulated me through the branches of the tree, but he did very gently suggest to the tree, and to me through the tree that I shape myself in more beautiful, harmonious directions.

In awe, I ventured to ask a question that was still in my mind, "Is there really a place in China or Japan where priests learn disciplines to respond to every situation in life?"

He said to me, "There may be such a place as a mystery school, but you are already enrolled in the highest of mystery schools on the planet."

"He told me a story of a young man at a School of the Mysteries waiting for classes to start. As he left his room and walked down the hallway to the dining room, he noticed a broom leaning against a wall with some dust in the hallway and he thought, "Someone has not finished their work and the place is a mess. This is no way to run a mystery school."

He had his meal, came back and noticed that the dirt and broom were still there. He went back to his room and meditated, still waiting for the classes to start. After his afternoon meditation, he went again to the dining room for dinner. The broom and the dirt remained untouched, and now there was a mop and bucket parked against the opposite wall. He thought, "How careless. I thought this school was the best available." Irritated, he went to eat. As expected, when he returned, the mess in the hallway remained. "I am going to tell somebody about this," he muttered. "In fact, I am not sure I want to stay here. If the masters of this school do not have it together any better than this, they cannot teach me very much." And he was still waiting for the lessons to begin.

This story was meant to illustrate the Planetary Mystery School. It is not possible for you to need a lesson without the lesson appearing. The next lesson is always before you. Teachers can help you see the lessons. That is their purpose. But teachers come in many disguises. No waitress was ever unkind to you in a restaurant without a reason. No cashier ever was impatient or short with you without purpose. No husband or wife or child ever put you through trauma when you did not need it. You already study at the feet of a perfect teacher if you listen to your Inner Teacher and to what life is saying to you. The mop and bucket are before you.

You have a lesson where you are. Whatever the lesson is, it is in your path and you have one of two choices — to pick up the mop, or to push it out of the way. Learn to recognize the next step along the path.

The only difference between people in the mystery school is that some are enrolled and sleep, while some wake up. We do not have the option of leaving the school. We do not have the option to resign the lessons. The only options are to learn the lessons or not. When we begin to participate and are enrolled on purpose, the lessons are more effective and life takes new meaning.

There may be Mystery Schools hidden in the deserts and forests of a remote land, teaching initiates to become Meta-Humans, but the mysteries learned in that exotic place are not greater. There is no greater school than The Planetary Mystery School.

CHAPTER XVI

What The Meta-Human Looks Like

Meta-Humans do exist. They are alive and well on this planet in our lifetime.

The four examples I offer here are not the only examples of Living Love in action today, but I believe they are four of the greatest. I refer to them not only as Meta-Humans, but as saints and masters. I don't use those terms loosely. They are saints because they are pure love alive. They are masters because they live their lives so effectively that magic and miracles are daily occurrences in their lives. Each of these people has influenced the course of history.

JIMMY YEN

At the turn of the century, there was a young boy in China who was taught the classics by his father through an ancient Chinese method. The two would shout the text of the classics as loud as possible, and as the boy learned the I Ching and the other ancient teachings his father said, "I see in this child the eyes of Confucius. He knew the text before I taught him."

The unique quality of Yang-chu Yen was both a blessing and a curse, because at age 10 his father told him, "I've given you the classics, but you have a destiny that goes beyond what I can teach you and what you can learn in our small community. You have to learn science and western thinking."

Yang-chu's father arranged for the boy to go to a school of western learning 90 miles away. The boy set out with his oldest brother, carrying only a small bundle. They walked rough trails through the wilderness for five days. They spent the nights in what were called "inns" but were more like barns. It was there the boy first encountered the other "species" of Chinese.

In China at that time, most of the people believed there were really two distinct species: those who could learn, and those who could not. Although poor, this boy and his family were among the more fortunate because of their ancestry. They were the "humans," who could study, learn, and improve themselves. The others were considered almost as beasts, a species separate from educated humans. There was no law that denied them an education; it was just accepted that they could not learn. None of them had ever tried. They were referred to by two Chinese characters, ku and li, which mean "bitter strength." Americans and Europeans adapted the Chinese sound or pronunciation to their own language and these people became known as "coolies."

When they stayed at an inn for the night Yang-chu and his brother would sit in a circle with several coolies, all soaking their sore feet in a common hot tub. The young boy listened intently to their stories. The coolies cursed and joked with one another as they told of carrying their heavy loads, much like truckers do in the United States today. The boy recognized something noble in them, and he began to care about them. His compassion for them would determine the direction of his entire life.

The boys completed their trek and arrived at the school late at night. They were greeted by an eccentric Englishman who ran the school. He held a lamp up to the Yang-chu's face and stared at him. "Such a small boy to enter this school!" he said. The older brother was told that he could not stay with his younger brother that night. The young boy was shown to his room, where he cried all night with terrible homesickness. The prefect heard him cry, and the next morning he said to the older brother, "This boy is too young to be at school. Take him home and come back in two or three years."

Yang-chu knew he could not return home. He could not fail and lose face. "Let me stay one more night," he said. "If I cry, send me home. If I make it, let me go to the school." The teacher agreed, and that night the boy stuffed a corner of the quilt in his mouth to muffle his homesick sobs. He was allowed to stay. The boy did well in school and after four years, at age 14, he was granted a scholarship to a high school run by American missionaries. This time the boy had to walk 200 miles get to the school. It was a 14 day journey that he made alone, again spending nights in inns with coolies and farmers, listening to the lives of common men.

At age 17 Yang-chu graduated at the top of his class. While in high school he found a friend, an Englishman named James Stewart. Because of the prejudice at the school toward the Chinese, James Stewart had started a youth hostel so the native boys would feel comfortable in their home environment. Yang-chu lived at the hostel and interpreted for

James. James encouraged his studies until it was time to show him more of the world. They traveled together 40 days to Hong Kong to see James's older brother, Arthur. The boy was so grateful for James's kindness that he called himself from then on Yang-chu James Yen. His American friends would call him Jimmy, Jimmy Yen.

Arthur Stewart enrolled James Yen in a college preparatory school, where he completed a three year course of study in one year. He received the highest grade on the exam and won a scholarship to study at Hong Kong University. He could not keep it, however, because he would not renounce his Chinese citizenship. He went to the university anyway, working his way through, but finding the British imperialistic attitude unbearable, he left.

An American missionary helped him raise money to go to Oberlin College in the United States. However, during the boat voyage he met a Yale graduate who encouraged him to apply at Yale University. When the dean of Yale asked him how much money he had, James said $84. "You are a brave young man," the dean said, and admitted him to the junior class. Jimmy loved Yale, though he had to work very hard to maintain his studies and pay his own way. In his second year he won a full scholarship to continue.

In 1918, the year Jimmy graduated from Yale, he was drawn into a bizarre scene that most history books neglect to include. In France during World War I casualties on the front lines were appalling, and the Allies needed manpower. They began to transport coolies from China to replace Allied laborers who were doing construction and supply work, so more soldiers would be available to fight at the front lines.

The British recruited a horde of poor, ragged coolies with promises of daily food and wages. None of them knew where they were going or what they would be doing. Each one went through the "sausage machine," where his pigtail was chopped off, his clothes were burned, he was deloused, finger-printed, and given a metal wristband with a number.

By the time Jimmy Yen graduated from Yale, there were nearly 180,000 coolies in France. It was wet and cold. The soldiers drove the coolies like slaves for 10 hours a day, and they could not digest the unfamiliar "Western" food. Many turned to drink and drugs, sold to them by profiteering maimed ex-soldiers. The coolies became sick, angry, depressed and lonely. They had been told they would not be fighting, but many were moved to the front lines to handle live ammunition in the trenches, and some were required to dig up and rebury dead British and French soldiers who had been placed in temporary graves. Needless to say, riots and strikes were common in these "Chinese Labor Corps."

The YMCA invited Jimmy to France to help make the lives of the coolies more bearable. Jimmy agreed because of his love for them, and two days after graduation he was on the boat. He was put in charge of a Y canteen at the Boulogne camp, where he sold candy and cigarettes and organized games and entertainment. Jimmy quickly realized that the worst of the coolies' suffering was homesickness. Some of the men had been away from home for years and were out of touch with China, where family and local custom were the main focus of living. They knew that Jimmy could read and write, and began asking him to send letters home to their families.

The first night he wrote three letters, the next night there were 12 to write, and the next night 50. Word spread and soon there were 200 and 300 men waiting for Jimmy to write for them. With 5,000 men in the Boulogne camp, Jimmy knew he could not write for all of them.

Jimmy meditated on the problem and remembered an old proverb. "If you catch a man a fish, you feed him for a day. If you teach him how to fish, you'll feed him for a lifetime."

It seemed impossible. There were 3,000 complex characters in the Chinese dialect that Jimmy spoke. Knowing the coolies didn't use all of them when they spoke, he condensed the vocabulary to 600 common words for speaking and writing, and it seemed more possible. He received permission from the commanding officer to address the camp. He said, "I will not write letters for you anymore." They all laughed. They did not believe him. "You cannot do that to us," they thought. "It is our lifeline. You cannot stop writing letters."

"I'm serious," Jimmy said. "I will not write letters for you anymore, but if you are willing, I will teach you to write them yourselves." The laughter was even louder this time. It was inconceivable to them. In their minds, it was not a matter of learning the letters. Because of their cultural conditioning, they believed they would have to become a different species to read and write.

"It can be done," Jimmy insisted. "You can learn." He could not convince them, but he did get 40 men to volunteer for an experiment. They did not expect to learn to read, but they would indulge him. After ten hours of heavy labor, they would go to Jimmy for one hour a night, and he began to teach them the 600 Chinese characters. Together they began to change the 4,000-year-old course of Chinese history. After four months Jimmy gave them a test and 35 passed it. They could write.

Jimmy had these men write letters for hundreds of men, but the others still did not believe him. Maybe Jimmy was still writing the letters himself. So he painted a wall black and with chalk wrote the news of the day. He stood his students before the entire camp and had them read from the wall to the people. The coolies thought they were seeing magic, a miracle. In his next class, Jimmy had 2,000 students, too many for him to teach alone, so he trained coolies to teach other coolies to read and write. He called them "assistant professors." Soon there were 5,000 literate coolies, then 20,000, and by the end of the war there were 80,000.

The Tommies and doughboys went home, but the coolies stayed to clean up the ravaged battlefields. The director of the YMCA Chinese Labor Corps asked Jimmy to start an educational program for the 180,000 coolies still in France. Jimmy agreed and created a newspaper for the men in the camps to read, called *The Chinese Laborer's Weekly.*

Jimmy wanted to return to the United States and continue his education. His ambition was to become a Chinese politician and change the course of Chinese history by using the model of democracy as practiced in the United States.

One coolie's gift caused him to change his plan. "This newspaper that you are publishing is the lifeblood of China. You cannot stop publishing it," he pleaded. "The newspaper costs one cent a piece to print. I've saved 365 francs. Take it," he said. The coolie had been working in the trenches of France for three years at a salary of 2 francs a day. Because of the man's dedication, Jimmy decided to continue publishing his newspaper. He knew then that he would devote his life to the education of these people.

In 1920 the Chinese Labor Corps was finally dissolved, and Jimmy returned to the United States to study for a Masters Degree at Princeton. In his second year he gave up his scholarship to go back to China to see his ailing mother. He returned to his family hearth penniless and dressed like a coolie.

Assured that his mother was well, he went to Shanghai. He was convinced that the YMCA was the only organization that truly cared about the Chinese peasants. The YMCA director there asked Jimmy to start a department for popular education. While there he married Alice Huie, the daughter of a Presbyterian missionary from New York's China-town, who worked as an instructor at the YMCA.

With the help of Chinese graduates of Harvard and Columbia, Jimmy created a simple book called the People's Thousand-Character Reader. They chose Changsha, the capital of Hunan province, for their first literacy campaign, where they held a big parade with the slogan: "An illit-

erate man is a blind man." Jimmy had high school and college students
recruit the illiterate peasants, and local teachers volunteered to teach
them for an hour each evening. Almost 1,000 passed the first four-
month course and were awarded certificates from the governor of the
province on graduation day. Jimmy immediately initiated a second class
in Shanghai, and then started a second campaign target, Yantai, a
northern port city frequented by British and American ships. Here he
shocked the Chinese by enrolling girls and women. For thousands of
years only men had enjoyed the honor of being educated.

An aristocratic woman whose feet had been bound by custom pre-
sided at that first graduation. She wept, saying, "I have never before
seen barefoot scholars." She became Jimmy Yen's patroness and rallied
representatives from 20 provinces to help Jimmy educate the masses.
That first year he operated out of a small room with a budget of about
$1,000 and one part-time clerk. His salary was $50 a month. During the
next twenty years his people taught millions of poor men and women all
over China to read and write. And that was not all he did.

Jimmy learned much from his students. A ten-year-old girl cow
herder who walked into the city for reading lessons helped Jimmyrealize
that he would have to get out of the cities and into the countryside if he
wanted to help the majority of the people. One day a farmer said to him,
"I can read, but my stomach growls as much as my neighbor's who can
not read." Jimmy realized he had to do more than just teach the people
how to read. He must deal with their poverty and hunger, their job
problems, disease and bad government.

He realized that to help these people he would have to live as they
lived to win their trust. He persuaded 30 exceptional, highly-educated
people with expertise in education, agriculture, and medicine to leave
their comfortable homes in the city and join him in the mud huts of the
country.

They chose to start in the county of Ding Xian, which had 500 square
miles, 400,000 peasants, and 472 poor villages. The plan was to make a
shining example of Ding Xian for the rest of the 1,900 xians in China.

Jimmy and his team listened to what the people wanted and observed
what they needed. They set up a comprehensive four-part program to
deal with education, work, health and self-government. When the gentry
came to the peasants, it usually meant more taxes or new ways forced
upon them. The coolies were suspicious. But Jimmy and his team won
them over by showing the elders that they could make the illiterate
"blind" see in four months with only one hour a night of their time. As

Jimmy did in France, they found a few brave souls to begin the lessons, and the rest followed. Thousands learned to read.

In 1928 Jimmy went to the United States to accept an honorary degree from Yale and used the trip to raise a half-million dollars for his pilot programs. Henry Ford liked his large-scale vision and donated $10,000.

After teaching some of the peasants to read, the team set up "people's schools" in the villages and encouraged them to be self-supporting. When the people needed something to read, the team wrote daily "wall news" and later published a weekly paper called *The Farmer*.

Next they turned to the food program. Jimmy did not believe that imported fertilizers and chemicals would make the earth more productive. He found resources already present in the villages, and set up a compost system and natural gardening methods to increase the yield. This was the basis of the national system of agriculture, which is still used in China today. It is the most productive on the planet.

Next came health. Jimmy and his team began what is today the national medical system of China, sometimes called the "barefoot doctors." Jimmy did not try to bring in the allopathic medical methodology of the West. Instead, he went to the mysterious healers who practiced herbology, acupuncture, and nutrition, and persuaded them to explain the cause/effect relationships that resulted in people being healed. What had been seen as magic was demystified and made available to the people. "Barefoot doctors" were trained and went into the villages throughout China.

Last came government reform. Having learned to read, the coolies began to participate in the political process. They began to understand that they were being paid nothing for a great deal of work, so they began to unite and call a halt to local corruption. Jimmy appealed to the Chinese ideal of the family and presented the vision of all citizens living in harmony, each with an equal voice. Through democracy he saw that China could realize her ancient ideal: "Under heaven, one family."

Jimmy's peaceful existence in Ding Xian was disrupted by Japan's invasion of China in 1937. He used this turn of events to expand the scope of his work. The team moved to Changsha and he began applying his programs to the entire province of Hunan — population 30 million. His team initiated massive reforms before the Japanese forced him to move again. Reminiscent of the founders of the early church who were driven out of Jerusalem and had to take their message from city to city, Jimmy was driven from province to province by the invading Japanese.

Jimmy and his followers went from community to community with their teachings, as people became literate throughout China.

Jimmy's reputation widened and respect for him grew, though not always with positive results. One warlord offered to organize the people of his state and make Jimmy its ruler. He refused, and the warlord became angry. He came to arrest Jimmy, who was in another province at the time, so he arrested his top assistant instead, a man named Chin.

When Jimmy returned and learned what had happened, he was furious and went directly to the prison. There he found Chin sitting in a cell with two guards. Chin had a stick, and he was scratching Chinese characters in the dirt. The guards were learning how to read, and when Jimmy and Chin left, they cried. Notice the way Meta-Humans work. When they don't have hospitals or schools, they pick up a stick and write in the dirt to change people's lives, and in so doing, they change the course of history.

Next Jimmy took on the whole political system of China, but he was running out of time. He started the College of Rural Reconstruction in his native Sichuan province, and after Japan's defeat in 1946 he was eager to sell his plan for educating the country to General Chiang Kai-shek. But Chiang was preoccupied with fighting the Communist leader Mao Tse Tung, rumored to be one of Jimmy's early literacy teachers.

In 1947, Jimmy traveled to the United States to enlist support from Congress. In 1948, Congress appropriated $27 million for his Rural Reconstruction program. But Jimmy would only spend $4 million of it before the Communists took over in 1949. Finally, after he taught millions of coolies in China to read and write, Jimmy was driven from his homeland.

But he didn't stop. From a funding base in the United States he began to help educate the poor throughout the rest of the world. He said, "Every third world country has illiterates like the coolies. Something must be done about it."

He went first to the Philippines, where college students volunteered for work in the barrios with the slogan: "Go to the people. Live among them. Learn from them. Plan with them. Start with what they know and build on what they have." In a few years his rural reconstruction teams had covered all the islands. As a result, in 1956 the first national elections were held. In 1960, Jimmy founded the International Institute for Rural Reconstruction (IIRR), which began to train students from other Third World countries. Jimmy's ideas were adapted to native cultures throughout the 1970s and 1980s. He traveled to India, Guatemala,

Ghana, Columbia, Kenya, Bangladesh, Sri Lanka, Nepal, Thailand, and Indonesia, finding teachers. He helped them put together primers for reading, agriculture, medicine, and for participating in the political process. Jimmy Yen has changed the course of history. At age 94, he was still working.

He was once asked, "Is your ambition, your goal, your ideal to change the course of history?"

Jimmy said, "There is only one ideal worthy of any man, and that is to be the Christ."

(During the preparation of this manuscript we learned that Jimmy Yen passed away. It is an honor to be able to include his inspiring example in this book, and we believe the highest tribute we can pay him is to follow that example, aspiring to be Meta-Humans.)

MR. EDHI

I know less about the life of this Meta-Human, but what I do know is enough to recognize him as one of the greatest men now living. When Abdul Sattar Edhi was 16 he had a fifth grade education and was working in a garment factory. He was deeply pained to see his mother suffering. She was crippled and mentally ill, despised by relatives and ridiculed by strangers.

The son had no money, but he made a solemn vow to help his mother. He did not know what to do or where to start. Day by day he cared for her, and then he began to help others, especially the sick, and those who were poor and abandoned who had no one else to help them. Because he was uneducated, his efforts were small and simple but practical. Someone gave him an old, beat-up abandoned ambulance, in which he drove around and picked up abandoned people who were sick or hungry. Others liked what he was doing, and after a while they began giving him money to help with his work.

His work is still simple and practical, but it is no longer small. Now (1990) Mr. Edhi is 58 and directs a foundation that accepts no corporate donations or government funds, but receives more than $5 million a year from private donations and provides a welfare net that is bigger than that of the Pakistani government welfare system. He runs 50 welfare centers, with free clinics, maternity wards, pharmacies and huge 1,200-bed shelters. He serves mental patients, heroin addicts, battered wives, orphans and runaways. There are several centers in Karachi and in 10 other cities, also a dozen emergency outposts along the national highway. He now has 200 ambulances, four times what the Karachi government health system has, and has purchased the country's first civilian rescue helicopter.

Mr. Edhi has a flowing white beard and wears workman's clothes. He doesn't bother to give a public accounting of his funds. "What need?" he says. "Do I live like a rich man? Look at me. Now go look at our projects. You will see where the money goes."

He has rescued 1,300 abandoned children, which has angered religious leaders. "They tell me it is against Islam," he says. "Some of the mullahs say these children are a sin against Allah, a defilement. Well, I am religious, too. But I won't enter discussion with the mullahs and the orthodox on this. They are narrow-minded. Their ideology is too short. All religions teach the help of mankind. Which one does not say the same? Anyway, the girls come to us in the night with their babies. They leave no name or address. What to do?"

The Edhi Home in Apnagar fosters social change. Young girls and beaten wives who live there are angry with a society that gives men permission to abuse their wives. One young woman who is seeking a divorce from her husband said, "My father and brothers beat me and force me to marry an old man. I will fight to get a divorce. I will get other women to fight with me. We will fight together." An Edhi aide said, "I know I shouldn't say it, but that is just the kind of attitude we like. Women have a bad deal in this country. Girls like that? Who knows, maybe they can change things."

Many ambulance drivers are orphans who came out of the huge Korangi Children's Center outside Karachi, which houses and educates 900 children. These ambulance drivers are becoming local legend as they rescue people, animals and even birds in need. "It is sad to see the lost ones," said a driver. " We find them helpless, or people call us to take them away."

The drivers have also recovered, washed and buried 20,000 unclaimed corpses. Polaroid snapshots of these corpses cover the walls outside Mr. Edhi's Karachi headquarters. "They die all alone and no one cares," says Mr. Edhi. "So we take their picture, and hope maybe someone will know them."

Poor people come with small amounts to give Mr. Edhi, and the well-dressed also come, sometimes with larger amounts. Why? "Because Edhi serves our people," says a businessman.

SISTER AGNES

One of the most famous living Meta-Humans was born in 1910 in

Yugoslavia, the daughter of an affluent Albanian grocer. At age 18, she became a nun and was sent to the Himalayas to study. At 21, she was assigned to teach in an upper-class girl's school in Calcutta, where she soon became the principal. The girls were dressed in clean, starched uniforms and were well-taught.

Sister Agnes was assigned a room above the high wall that surrounded the well-endowed school, and from her window she could see the slum below. She could look down at the dirt street with its open, running sewer, and she could watch the children beg and steal to support their families.

Sister Agnes watched for years, until one day she could no longer stand it. She sat down to eat her meal in the cafeteria with the girls, looked at the food, and couldn't eat it. She picked up her plate and walked outside the compound. The girls were curious because they didn't know what she was doing.

The next day Sister Agnes again picked up her plate and walked out of the compound. This time two of the girls followed her and watched her give away her lunch to the children in the street. And the next day a stream of little girls in starched uniforms filed down the compound into the street to give their lunches away.

Day after day they gave their lunches away, but it wasn't enough for Sister Agnes. She went with the girls to the hospitals and clinics to beg for bandages and medicine, and they brought them to the people of the streets throughout Calcutta.

Riding a train to Darjeeling in 1946 she felt a clear call from God. "Leave the convent and help the poor. Live among them." She says it was an order from God.

She wrote the Church and applied to become a "free nun." It was a radical concept at that time. If her application were granted, she would have to leave the convent and, with no material support from the Church, go out on her own. She felt she had to go out and live among the people, because she thought, "If I'm going to make a change, I have to affirm their lives by living as they do."

After two years she finally received permission, and left the convent with a small amount of subsistence money. She could have used the money to rent a storefront building, to set up a school or clinic, or perhaps to travel to Yugoslavia to raise money for the people. She didn't. She spent the little money she had on a paramedic course.

Now a paramedic, with no food, money, or place to live, she went back to the street with the open sewers. She didn't worry about those things. She picked up a stick and began to scratch letters in the dirt. The children gathered around her and she began to teach.

At the end of the day, the children dispersed. Sister Agnes had no place to stay, so she wrapped her sari around her and laid down under a tree. The people of the slum watched her with curiosity, wondering what she would do. They couldn't believe she would just sleep under a tree, but she was still lying there as it became dark. Finally, someone came out of a little hut and asked, "Won't you at least sleep on the floor?" She went inside.

They were ashamed to give her the food that they ate because they couldn't imagine her eating out of a common pot. They apologized for not having food to give her. Sister Agnes looked in the pot and said, "That looks good. I'll have some. I'm very hungry." So they fed her.

Soon, in 1949, one of the girls from the convent school came to Sister Agnes and said, "I am leaving the school. I have to do this with you." Now there were two, and that meant an order had been founded. Sister Agnes became Mother Theresa, and her student became Sister Agnes. Sister Agnes is still Number 2 in the Missionaries of Charity, the new order which formally began in October 1950. Other nuns joined them, and they established clinics and schools for the poor and home- less in Calcutta.

Today the Missionaries of Charity has 3,000 nuns, 400 brothers, and centers all over the world.

They rescue babies from trash bins, where the poorest of the poor in India throw them away when the mothers are so emaciated that they cannot produce milk. The sisters fan out throughout the city, find the babies, house them and feed them. They find homes through adoption agencies for the healthy ones. Those who are severely retarded or crippled and need full-time care are kept and cared for by the sisters.

It was Christmas 1954 when Ann Blaikie, the wife of an English lawyer, heard of Mother Theresa's work. She wanted to help so she brought toys for the children to have a Christmas party. "The children need clothes," Mother Theresa said. Ann left the party and brought back clothes. "Now the Moslem children have to have a party with clothes and toys, and so do the Hindu children," Mother Theresa said. "I wasn't going to let her off the hook. God called Ann Blaikie just like He called me, and she can't just drop off some toys and go back to her comfortable life."

So they had a party for the Moslems and for the Hindus. Ann came back each day to help in the clinics and the schools, but one day she sent her chauffeur with a note that read, "I can't come in today. I have a fever." Mother Theresa wrote back, "I too have a fever, but it is better to burn in this world than the next." Ann came in and quietly went to work.

Ann Blaikie became the founder of a group called Co-Workers of Mother Theresa, now a world-wide organization with some three million volunteers that sets up centers and supports the work of the Sisters of Charity.

Mother Theresa came to England to visit the Society of Co-Workers and as she was walking through Trafalgar Square a heroin addict fell in front of her and died at her feet. She picked him up, summoned an ambulance, and had him brought to a hospital. She went to the co-workers and said, "Hear this. Your first responsibility is to build shelters for the drug addicts and for the destitute and dying in London."

The co-workers looked for a building to house the addicts, but they had no money. Mother Theresa found a suitable building herself. It was on the market for 9,000 British pounds, and she sent a note to the landlord offering 6,000. The landlord saw Mother Theresa's name on the note and accepted her offer, but they still had to find the 6,000 pounds. "How are we going to raise that much money?" they asked.

Mother Theresa set out with her big, open, knitting bag on her arm, with the knitting needles hanging out. "I'll be back in a few days," she said. Mother Theresa doesn't do fund raising. She just visited all of the co-workers throughout England carrying her bag. When she returned to London, she took the bag from her arm and said, "I think there's some money in here."

Ann's husband counted it. Then he took a five-pound note out of his pocket and said, "We have 6,000 pounds."

That's how a master works.

Mother Theresa returned to India. Her next project was to help the lepers. She found a strip of land along a railroad track owned by the railroad that wasn't being used. She applied to the railroad for it and was refused. So she rounded up all the lepers she could find, and with helpers who were not afraid to be with the lepers they moved onto the land.

"We can't give them money," she said. "They are already beggars. Do you want to encourage that as a lifestyle? What we have to do is teach them a trade." She found carpenters to work with the lepers to help them build a string of long, narrow buildings along the strip of railroad track. She had made carpenters out of lepers. When the railroad saw they had built permanent structures, they donated the land.

In those buildings, they gathered 50-year-old treadle-type sewing machines. She and her sisters and co-workers taught lepers, some with no hands or no feet, to make the saris that the nuns of her order wear all over the world. She taught them to make shoes, and a shoe manufacturing unit was added to the complex of little factories along the railroad tracks.

There now is a cure for leprosy and lepers can come there for treatment. When caught in the early stages, it can be cured completely. Even in advanced stages, although the deformities remain, the progression of the disease can be arrested.

Mother Theresa's home for the destitute and dying in Calcutta (Kaligat) has become a "must stop" for people from all over the world, particularly for young people. Some stay for a month, a year, two years, and some decide to devote their lives to her work and never leave.

It came about when Mother Theresa found a woman dying outside the entrance to a hospital where the indigent were turned away. The Sisters of Charity and Co-Workers now go to the doors of the hospitals of Calcutta each day, find the dying, and bring them to Kaligat. Many have only a short time to live, but in their last few hours someone holds their hands and comforts them.

The volunteers come from India, England, Canada, the United States, and around the world. They don't need training. The volunteers need only sit with the patients, let them know they care, hold their hands, sing to them. They feed them and change their beds. Some patients do recover, and when they do, many become permanent staff, and then they sit, and sing, and care for the patients in the same way they were nurtured.

Whether Christian, Moslem, Hindu, or Buddhist, there is no attempt to give them religious training. They save their lives and give them love.

Mother Theresa says, "We may not be able to feed them all, or give them jobs or an education, but there is one thing that people need not starve for, and that is love."

A young doctor who had become disillusioned with religion telling people how to "be good" became a volunteer at Mother Theresa's home for the destitute and dying. He wrote home and said, "I've never felt more alive than in this place of death. I have never known heaven, except in this hell. If every young man and woman in the world could come here and see this place and hold the hand of one of these people before they go out into the world and begin their profession, they would become compassionate individuals. I feel almost ashamed when people feel that I am serving these patients, knowing what they do for me."

SISTER EMMANUELLE

Twenty years ago when the Church told Sister Emmanuelle that it was time to retire, the 62-year-old French nun, a college professor teaching in Cairo, was upset. So she told God she'd go to the worst place on Earth, if He would let her keep working. God must have heard her because she ended up in Cairo's City of Garbage, surely one of the most hellish places on the planet. At least it used to be.

The City of Garbage is a slum outside Cairo, the hot, smoky, stinky home of some 30,000 outcasts who collect and live off the garbage. Every morning hordes of children go out with their donkey carts to collect some 2,000 tons of garbage from Cairo streets, and take it back to their City. For more than a hundred years they have lived there, completely cut off from society, the most detested people in Egypt. They make their hovels from the garbage, eat from it, dress from it, and feed it to their pigs, taboo animals in Moslem countries. They salvage what they can from the garbage — glass, paper, plastic — and sell it.

"I was the first human being to enter this place," says Sister Emmanuelle, who is learning to speak English. "Even the police are not going in there. They got knives. My friends said to me that they will kill me."

But she went in anyway, because God told her it was all right, and she began building a small tin-and-cardboard shelter from the garbage. She knew that to help these people she would have to live with them, to become like them. The children were amused at this strange lady building a new home from their garbage. They began helping her.

"I was so happy to marry the slum," she says. "The children cheered me when I came. 'El arroussah, el arroussah,' they said. Young bride. Of course, these people are despised. And that's the reason that I came here, TO share their lives, night and day, to prove to them that they are human beings, that they are sons and daughters of God."

Today Sister Emmanuelle is the saint of the City of Garbage, although she protests she is not a saint because she has a hot temper and is not patient enough. Now 82, the ex-college professor was once the privileged daughter of a wealthy businessman, who never thought she'd make it as a nun. "I was very coquette," she says.

She used her spiritual fire and charm to build schools, clinics, a compost factory, and houses for her people. She carefully manages the $6 million she raises from charities, to improve their lives. She is most proud of the new high school. She raised $1 million to build and staff it, and it now has 800 students.

Her own house is now bright green, a one room luxury suite. "My home is a palace, much better than a Hilton or a Sheraton," she says, though she still has no water and no electricity, and finds an occasional rat in her bed.

Though deeply compassionate, she has a firm rule that she will only help those who are willing to help themselves. No one gets a free ride around Sister Emmanuelle. "I don't give money to anybody," she says. "That's very bad to give money, because I don't want they will be beggars. Give me, give me, give me. Ah, that's awful!"

She helps the families who come up with a little money to build new houses, and she encourages them to keep their new homes clean. She rewards those who clean their homes with a picture of the Madonna. "A prize," she says, "because the room is so clean, so good, and I want that after one or two years maybe 150 families will have a nice clean house like that. Yes, dear, it will be."

She finds the children easiest to love, and they cling to her everywhere she goes. "But they are going without shoes," she says, concerned about the health hazards of bare feet in the garbage. "I told them so many times, you must have your shoes." Now she insists that no child gets to come to school without shoes.

"School is the most wonderful place for me," she says, "because you see the children are so happy. It's wonderful to be happy children." And she knows that each child she can educate has a chance to learn a profession that will lift them out of the City of Garbage. It's a tough fight, because many parents want the children to stay there and collect garbage, because it's the only way they know.

After the children she cares most for the women. Sister Emmanuelle calls them "beaten slaves." On their wedding night the young brides are tested by the old women for virginity, with blood on the cloth for proof. If the woman isn't a virgin, she gets beaten and sometimes even killed. The women bear children, sort the garbage, and often get beaten by their husbands. At first Sister Emmanuelle tried to get the women to rebel against their husbands, but they were just beaten more, so she changed her tactic.

The old coquette now slyly charms the men. She humors the men into making promises not to beat their wives, at least for a day or a week. "That's very important to do because everybody's looking at him and they told him now you have not to do that. And slowly, slowly I think that perhaps one week he will not beat. And at the end of the week I am going to say, 'Ah, your promise, yes, and now a new promise for the next week.' Slowly, slowly, slowly, slowly. The men are most difficult to change. You can change the women, but the men, very difficult. But it will change by the school."

Sister Emmanuelle tells the story of the great temptation in her life. "Once it was a teacher, a very, very clever, good-looking teacher, a man." He was a philosophy professor, and she cried long and hard wrestling with the decision to stay a nun. On the day she celebrated 50 years of being a nun, she got a letter from this man. "It was a very nice letter, offer congratulations, and my heart was doing some noise. I could have had children like the garbage collectors: one, two, three, four, five, six, seven, eight, nine, ten, eleven. And now I am the mother of a thousand children. Is it not better?"

In Sister Emmanuelle's room is a picture of people dancing together in joy. "I have in my home the dance of the people who are going to heaven. We are going like that, up, up, up to heaven. That's absolutely marvelous, and that's my life. I am dancing with my people to have a nicer life and to go, to go, to go to God."

I offer you these four people, Jimmy Yen, Mr. Edhi, Mother Theresa, and Sister Emmanuelle, as evidence that Living Love is alive and well today on this planet.

CHAPTER XVII

The Laws Governing Reality

AGREEMENTS — NOT THE BARS OF A PRISON

*"It may seem frustrating, even paradoxical that the
only people who can really produce miracles are those
who possess such qualities of character, the endless
patience and boundless acceptance of law to find
no need for miracles."*

The evidences of Meta-Human character are impeccable honesty,
integrity that is absolute, and unconditional love. The Master Jesus
taught that if one could keep "the whole law" as given by Moses, He
would have these qualities of character. He then "who is there among
you who has never broken one of these laws?" He accurately observed
that trying to keep rules and laws is not the way to build character.

In the United States today there is an argument among educators
and concerned Senators about teaching morals and morality in public
schools. There are those who insist that it must be done. Others argue
that morals and ethics can't be taught; they must be "instilled in the
individual's upbringing." Values, they say, are established in the formative years. When the child reaches the education system, it is too late to
"instill" value systems.

THE KEYS TO DEVELOPMENT OF CHARACTER

Love yourself, others and God, equally. This was the "new mystery"
that Christ taught. This, He said, is the whole law. This law does not
suggest loving others or even God more than yourself.

Love is the foundation for a powerful person who is capable and willing to accept responsibility for every word, action and thought, whose
acts are kind, supportive and understanding and who feels confident and
supported in meeting the challenges of life.

Having built an experiential, personal relationship with God, this
powerful person knows that the action of natural law is supportive to his

life and purpose. He realizes that no circumstance can be a real block to the expression of his purpose. This harmony with law is the source of miracles.

MIRACLES

It might be important to consider why such miracles such as walking on water, teleportation, levitation and even instant healing are so rare, and why they must remain rare occurrences. We have agreed upon a set of laws. Upon our projection into this reality, we agreed to establish, recognize and maintain a set of laws that govern this reality and make it coherent. If we each could cancel the effect of these laws at will, especially as a result of frustration, anxiety and the inability to cope with reality, we certainly would create a loss of coherent reality that would make all of us unable to cope.

In one particular ancient Mystery School the admonition was, "Obey the law that you might be able to overcome the law." In this school, the application of that teaching was followed in this way:

A group of healers were carefully trained in herbology, therapeutic massage, hydrotherapy and dry heat therapy, along with various other healing applications. The training was rigorous and the student healers conscientious.

The healer's initiation consisted of going out to the city gates where the ill were left outside the city walls. There was a great fear of spreading dread disease if the sick were allowed inside the city. Food was sometimes left by loved ones who might see their sick relatives only from great distances. If a loved one made contact with the sick they were considered unclean (infected) and were, themselves, ostracized, left beyond hope of making a living or even of feeding themselves.

The healer-initiates were sent to deliberately expose themselves to one patient (or sometimes more than one) then, being considered unclean, both healer and patient were isolated from others in the Mystery School and from the public. The healer lived with the patient in a cliff-wall cave, where they were sustained by food and supplies lowered by rope. The healer was deliberately giving his life for the life of the patient. The healer made a commitment to spend the rest of his life serving the health and survival needs of the patient.

The healer-initiates (called the therapeutae) discovered that patients often recovered even before they could be brought back to the Mystery School of healing. The belief was that when a healer has given, without reservation, the months or years of devoted time and energy required to nurse a patient to health, that time and energy may be transferred in an instant. According to their stories, the therapeutae could perform "instant healing miracles," not by attempting to heal instantly, but by giving years of their lives transmitted through an instantaneous commitment.

These same initiates reported that if one were traveling through a desert where no water is available and should encounter a person whose injuries require cool water, a similar effect could be produced using leaves, plant juice or even hot sand. But, they reported, the effect could only be produced by a conscientious healer who had studied hydrotherapy to understand the effects being sought.

These initiates were people who understood, obeyed and respected the law and thereby gained the natural support of the law while overcoming the law's limitation.

NO NEED FOR MIRACLES

It may seem frustrating, even paradoxical, that the only people who can really produce miracles are those who possess such endless patience and boundless acceptance of law they find no need for them. But we are fortunate that it is so.

Even those of us with "least character" have sufficient creativity to make things "bad or good" and to make ourselves or others "right or wrong." This creativity may be applied with sufficient energy to make absolutely sure that the condition is real. If a creative person is reasonable enough, others will agree that the condition is real. The good-bad, right-wrong quality judgments can even be applied to reality with sufficient force to create illness and other disasters.

Both individuals and even nations indulge blaming and making others wrong in order to be right. People, both individually and in groups, are willing to punish those they judge to be wrong. This willingness to judge and punish justifies a further willingness to deliberately cause pain and hurt.

If the ability to produce miracles was dependent upon anything so simple as wishing, positive thinking, or "willing it to be so," reality would not be sufficiently coherent to allow us to walk. Frustrated people, unwilling to accept results of their own thought and action would be "hardening" water to walk on it while others are trying to swim. Healers would arbitrarily abort natural biological processes for some, while others would "beam" their wrath to cause illness in those they wanted to punish. Research would, of course, be hopeless in an atmosphere where the constants upon which research depends are subject to "miracles."

143

A BALANCE OF POWER

There is evidence that our thoughts are powerful, even at a distance. It is known that "sympathetic sickness," in which a woman's pregnancy "morning sickness" is experienced by her man, can occur even when he is not physically present with her. There are good indications that the healing influence of caring can be communicated without physical touch.

The power of both curses and blessings of shaman and voodoo practitioners is well documented. The fact that such curses can produce fever and even death is credited to the power of suggestion. The "explanation" is almost comical when the critic then disclaims "faith healing." Little significance is attached to the fact that no shaman is recognized as such until he has produced evidence of his power. Shamen, in most cultures, endure years of training and apprenticeship as long and demanding as physicians. However, this does not count for much to the critic. But it is this point that must be considered. If the "power of thought" is available to the average person, it is made more effective by one who ardently trains to hone and concentrate it. The average person maintains a "balance of power" to counteract the suggestions of others (including beneficial or healing suggestions) but he is likely to be ineffective against a powerful shaman or other trained minds.

LOVE IS MORE POWERFUL THAN FEAR

We are fortunate that the paths of power are difficult and are mastered by few. We are even more fortunate that love is more powerful than fear. We are not helped by a belief that everyone who seeks to develop spiritual or mental power is evil. Such beliefs feed fear and tilt the balance of power in the wrong direction.

The paths of power are available to all those sufficiently disciplined and motivated to claim the tools of power. All of these tools, save one, may be used for good or evil. It is that one, the power of love, that determines whether a powerful being may be a Meta-Human.

"Though I speak with the tongues of men and of angels and have not love, I am become as sounding brass or a tinkling cymbal. And though I have the gift of prophecy, and understand all mysteries, and all knowledge; and though I have all faith, so that I could remove mountains and have not love, I am nothing."

"And though I bestow all my goods to feed the poor and though I give my body to be burned, and have not love, it profiteth me nothing."

"Love is long suffering and kind; love envieth not; love vaunteth not itself, is not puffed up, doth not behave itself unseemly, seeketh not her own, is not easily provoked, thinketh no evil; rejoiceth not in iniquity, but rejoiceth in the truth; beareth all things, believeth all things, hopeth all things endureth all things. Love never fails; but where there be prophecies they shall fail; where there be tongues they shall cease; where there be knowledge, it shall vanish away. For we know in part and we prophesy in part. But when that which is perfect is come, then that which is in part shall be done away."

"And now abideth faith, hope, love, these three; but the greatest of these is love." (I Corinthians 13: 1-10, 7-13)

Footnotes

CHAPTER 2

1. Houston, Jean, J. **The Possible Human.** Jean Houston, Ph.D., noted lecturer and author.

2. "Omni," Page 44, November 1984.

3. Lorayne, Harry, H. **The Memory Book**. New York, Stein and Day, 1974.

4. Wood, Evelyn, E. **Reading Dynamics.**

5. Hatha Yoga consists of a series of body postures called asanas.

6. Walter, C.G. **The Living Brain.** London, Penguin, 1961.

7. Watson, Lyall, L. **Super Nature.** New York, Anchor Press, Doubleday, 1973.

8. Shattuck, E.H. **Mind Your Body.** England, Turnstone Press Limited, 1979.

9. Edgar Cayce, called "The Sleeping Prophet," is widely known for his psychic readings.

10. Clark, Patrick, P. **Sports First.** New York, Facts on File, 1981.

11. Rowes, Barbara, B. "Omni." "Fighting Chance." p.80-86, November 1984.

12. Ibid.

13. Ibid.

14. Neel, David, D. **Magic and Mystery in Tibet**. London, Souvenir Press, 1967.

CHAPTER 3

1. With apologies to Dr. Jean Houston, Phd., for creating a third category which may seem to suggest "oneupmanship" on her term The Possible Human. Many of the attributes encouraged in her vision of The Possible Human are those I am here assigning to a third category, The Meta-Human. I use this third category to distinguish between the development of potential attributable to the human and that which may be attributed to metamorphosis.

    Houston, Jean, J. **The Possible Human.** California, J.P. Tarcher, Inc, 1979.

CHAPTER 4

1. Maltz, Maxwell, M. **Psycho-Cybernetics.** NJ, Prentice Hall, 1960.

2. Ignaz Semmelweis, a Hungarian physician who pioneered surgical antisepsis.

3. McMillan Dr. **None of These Diseases.** Revell Ca., N. J. 1974.

4. Jose Silva is founder of The Silva Method.

5. Ibid.

6. Burr, Dr. Harold Saxton, HS. **The Fields of Life.** New York, Ballantine Books, 1973.

7. Burr, Dr. Harold Saxton, H.S. **Blueprint for Immortality.** New York, Ballantine Books, 1973.

8. Russell, Edward, E. W. **Design for Destiny**. New York, Ballantine Books, 1973.

9. Hall, Manly. M. P. **Invisible Records of Thought and Action.** California, The Philosophical Research Society Inc., 1959.

10. The Edgar Cayce Readings #1549-L.

11. Houston, Jean, J. **The Possible Human. California,** J.P. Tarcher, Inc, 1979.

12. Krieger, Dolores, D. **The Therapeutic Touch.** NJ, Prentice Hall, 1979.

CHAPTER 5

1. St. John 1:51.

2. St. John, 3:1-21

CHAPTER 6

1. I Corinthians 6:19

2. Dawkins, Richard. **The Selfish Gene.** England, Oxford Press, 1976.

3. The Kabala is the ancient Hebraic esoteric teachings.

4. Dr. Derald G. Langham, Ph.D., a geneticist who is founder of "Genesa," author of many books including a series called **Genesa: Tomorrow's Thinking Today.**

5. Psalms 51:5

6. St. John, 10:34

7. I Corinthians 15:20

CHAPTER 7

1. Psalms 103: 10-12

2. I John 1:9

CHAPTER 13

1. Ostrander, Sheila & Schroeder, Lynn. **Super-Learning.** Dell Publishing Co., Inc., 1981.

2. Robert Monroe, The Monroe Institute, Rt. 1, Box 175, Faber, VA 22938

3. A Sanskrit word meaning "wheel," or vortex or energy related to a particular endocrine center of the body.

4. St. Luke 11:34